KDP

HOW TO SELF - PUBLISH YOUR

BOOK ON AMAZON

The Beginner's Guide

The key elements for
Independent

(Indie) author success

Ged Cusack

DISCLAIMER

This publication is designed to provide competent and reliable information regarding the subject matter covered. However, it is sold with the understanding that the author and the publisher are not engaged in rendering legal, financial or other professional advice. Laws and practices often vary from state to state and country to country and if legal or expert assistance is required, the services of a professional should be sought. The author and publisher specifically disclaim any liability that is incurred from the use or application of the contents of this book.

The publisher does not have any control over and does not assume any responsibility for author of third party websites and their content.

Contents

Introduction

From the outset of this book, I want you to realize that when you publish your own book, it is not only your creative masterpiece, but it is also a product!

This might come as a shock to some authors but whether you perceive yourself as an artist or a craftsperson, you are still creating a product for sale.

As you read this book your two main aims should be:

- To increase the visibility of your book, by getting it in front of more readers.
- To ensure that the readers get a great experience once they find your book.

The Kindle Direct Publishing (KDP) platform provides an opportunity for almost anyone to publish a Kindle book.

This book is written to focus you on the key elements required to successfully publish your book and sell it as a Kindle eBook.

There is a reason that there is no specific chapter in this book with the title "Marketing".

From the first moment you tell someone that you are writing a book, to the time your book is earning revenue, every element of your book production involves some aspect of marketing.

Lots of authors are introverts and see marketing as scary or something unpleasant.

Whenever I think of book marketing, I like to remember a short quote, by one of the most successful Indie authors out there today. Joanna Penn is also a self-professed introvert.

"Marketing your book is sharing what you love, with people who look forward to hearing about it." — ***Joanna Penn***

Your Book

Although there are many reasons why people write, I am going to assume that if you are reading this book, you want to publish your writing with KDP and you also want people to read it.

As an independent (Indie) author you are not just responsible for typing words on a page. You are accountable for a lot of the activities that a traditional publishing house would usually undertake (for their traditionally published authors).

Ultimately every element of your book's publication will have an impact on how successful it is received and sells. For the purpose of this book, we will class an element as either a physical part of your book or an activity, related to the book publishing process.

Just as many established six-figure traditional authors have books that end up in the bargain bins, Indie authors may also have books that just don't sell.

Fortunately, Indie authors have a lot of control over their book.

How to use this book

Layout

The layout of this book is such that someone new to publishing can start at the beginning and work through the process using the book as their guide.

- Determining your budget, identifying your target audience and planning your schedule are all activities that should be looked at early on in the process.
- The content of your book is a critical element but knowing how important the book cover and title are to attract your readers is also key.
- The chapters are crammed with useful guidance on the KDP Platform and I have also provided appendixes at the back of the book with separate checklists and templates.
- For those readers that have purchased this book as an eBook (or have the print version but don't want to write in it), I have created separate PDF versions of those appendixes.
- To access these PDFs, just visit my website at gedcusack.com and you can download them directly.

Reading Choices

As the publishing process is not totally linear, you will no doubt want to revisit chapters.

For any authors approaching this book later in your publishing journey, even if you feel the urge to dive into the later chapters, I still encourage you to read this guide from start-to-finish.

As an avid learner even I find many useful gems in books on subjects that I am already proficient.

Some people are skim readers and some people are methodical readers.

- If like me you are a skim reader, you may decide to have a quick read through the whole book, without doing any of the exercises. This is one of the reasons, I have included an appendix at the back of the book with a consolidation of all of the exercises.
- For the benefit of the methodical readers, the book is laid out as a companion to accompany you on your publishing journey.

There are many reasons why a book doesn't sell and although the contents in this book will not guarantee that your book will sell, it will give you a better fighting chance than just throwing some words on a page and hoping for success.

Chapter 1 Your Commitment

"When you know what you want and you want it badly enough, you'll find a way to get it." — **Jim Rohn**

The focus of this chapter is to help you determine what you have available (in both time and money) to commit to the business venture of your book.

In order to set you up with a strong foundation, you must accept right now that it will require a commitment of both your time and your money.

Whether you are focused on selling books as a supplemental income or as your main business, you still need to treat it as a business.

Although some authors may glaze over at the mention of writing as a business, you are not one of those authors. You are reading this book because you want your own book to succeed and like any business venture, Cashflow is its lifeblood.

Your initial writing commitment may primarily be time but as you progress through to the editing and marketing phases of publishing, there will be some financial requirements.

Even though there are books on the market with titles such as "Penniless publishing", you will have to commit some finances to this process. If like many independent authors, you are writing alongside paid employment, a strategic investment of some of your wages can expedite your publishing success.

Potential Expenditures

Before we start to assess where you are at in terms of your available resources, here's an overview of some of the potential areas that they will be required:

- Content creation.
- Book editing.
- Book formatting.
- Book cover design.
- Distributing Advanced Review Copies (ARCs) of your book.
- Book launching.
- Book Ads.

Time Requirements

Only you can decide how much time to allocate to your book, but if you have never written before it may take longer than you expect.

There is a balancing act between how much time you allocate to any project and the ability to maintain its momentum. One of the reasons that so many authors fail to complete their book, is that they don't maintain this balance.

Some fiction writers may take a year or more before they publish a novel and some writing machines like Chris Fox can produce a book in a few weeks. I highly recommend Chris's book "5000 Words Per Hour" if you are new to writing, or need some ideas on speeding up your content production.

Financial Requirements

If you start off with an idea of what your budget is, it can save you a lot of future stress on your publishing journey.

Because there are several steps in the publishing process, you don't necessarily need to spend your whole financial budget right away.

This means that you can begin the process with a smaller budget and add to it as you progress.

Knowing that you have a limited budget can also inspire you to use some "outside the box" thinking to make your book a success.

If you are planning to build your budget as you go, ensure that you schedule in your future costs. If you suddenly reach the early stages of your launch schedule and you don't have your marketing funds, it may force delays or even cancellation of your launch. Don't allow bad planning to halt your book's progress.

"Procrastination loves some justification." — ***Ged Cusack***

Allocation and Estimation of your Budget

If you are serious about publishing your work, you need to determine what time and money you have available and then allocate some specific amounts to your writing budget.

When allocating your time and money, you should always factor in some flexibility.

If you don't have any idea how much time and money you are going to need for your book, how can you know when it will be ready (and how can you estimate launch schedules, etc.)?

Later in the book, you will find further breakdowns of launch schedules and financial expenditure but at this initial stage of the process, you need to start laying out a tracking system for your budget.

We all have our preferences of Apps or software programs for tracking (whether you choose google docs, excel spreadsheets, etc.) here are some suggested headings for you to use:

- Initial time budget.
- Daily allocation of writing time.
- Initial financial budget.
- Estimated research time.
- Estimated total writing time for the first draft.
- Estimated editing costs (time).
- Estimated editing costs (financial).
- Estimated promotion costs (time).
- Estimated promotion costs (financial).

Tips to Maximize Your Time Efficiency

There are numerous books and courses on time management and it is not my intention to get into the discussion of whether we can multitask or not (Spoiler alert we can't).

Whether you are being inefficient through lack of sleep, unhealthy diets or for any other reason, it will have a negative impact on your productivity.

The focus of this section is to offer a few suggestions for making the most of your writing time:

- Eat Healthily – Most of us are aware that the food that we put in our mouth is the fuel for the engine that drives our body.

  With so many books, courses and even organizations out there dedicated to diet, I would not dream of telling you what the right food for you is. One comment I will make is that we tend to know which foods give us more energy and which feel like they are draining us. Try choosing foods that will increase your energy and not deplete it.

- Get the right amount of sleep – We vary in our sleep requirements and as indie authors, we may be writing before or after another full-time job.
One factor found to be an inhibitor for sleep is the blue light emitted from televisions, smartphones, and tablets, etc. The blue light suppresses melatonin and it is recommended that you reduce the exposure to this blue light, one to two hours before bed.

  If you need to be in front of a screen before bed here are two suggestions:
  - o Wear blue light blocking glasses (these are similar to the yellow lensed night driving glasses). You can buy them quite cheaply on Amazon.

  - o Use the inbuilt filters on your devices. iPads and iPhones have an option in the devices' "Display & Brightness" setting called "Night Shift". You can schedule this to automatically switch over during set hours of the night and the "Warmer" you position the setting, the more blue light is filtered out. For Macs and Android phones, you can download F.Lux and other options.

- Batching – Grouping together activities into separate categories, such as editing and marketing, can maximize the use of your time. Because it can take some time to switch from one mindset to another, it is more efficient to focus on activities in the same area.

- Dictation – With dictation software accuracy improving all of the time, two-finger typists like myself can increase the daily word count on their first draft considerably. I have an old version of "Dragon Home", a speech recognition software that I had almost given up on, due to my strong Yorkshire accent. After hearing Scott Baker's accent while he was being interviewed on "The Creativepenn" podcast (about using dictation), I used his tips to train my version of Dragon and achieved great results.

- Transcription – Some versions of Dragon (and other voice recognition) software allow you to dictate on your phone or digital recorder, they will then automatically transcribe your words into written text when you transfer the file to your computer.

  This added flexibility means that you can continue to work on your writing without being tethered to your computer. Some people advocate how cheap transcription services are, but I find (rather than ongoing transcription costs) a one-time purchase price for software is easier to work into my financial budget.

- Dictation Hybrid – Older versions of "Dragon" software (without the transcription option) can run on older computers. If you want to upgrade your software, you may have to upgrade your computer.

  If your current computer isn't of a high enough specification for "Dragon Premium" or "Dragon Professional" (which include the transcription function), there is a workaround. Record your dictation on a mobile device and then dictate the same information through your computer later, whilst simultaneously listening to the recordings through headphones. Although this isn't as efficient as transcription, it can still work out faster than typing and increase your time flexibility.

- Note-taking – If you have a busy brain like me, you may find that writing fast falls down, when you realize that your notes are illegible later on. I find that recording my notes in an audio format is a lot quicker (especially as I nearly always have my iPhone available).

A few things to consider here:

- o   If you are using a voice recorder app on your phone. Some apps constantly scan for background noise levels (even when you aren't recording). This scanning function can be a big drain on your phone's battery life. Unless I am actually recording I turn off the recording apps access to the microphone on my phone.

- o   Recording your notes is designed to improve efficiency. You must review the audio notes regularly or there is little point in recording this information.

Opportunity Costs

The image of a financially struggling artist can be most people's perception of a writer.

Even if we don't feel like we're struggling, we're either "Time Poor" or "Money Poor". Our lives will therefore, necessitate some trade-offs.

Wherever we decide to invest our time and money, we have determined that the potential return on our investment (R.O.I.) outweighs the opportunity cost. Because we can't invest the same resource in two different places the opportunity we are foregoing is the opportunity to invest elsewhere, that could provide a better R.O.I.

- •   If you are "Time Poor" but have money to invest in your book, the opportunity cost of using your money to invest in your book is that you reduce the ability to invest that same money in another venture. That other venture could produce a better (R.O.I.) for your money.

- If you are "Money Poor" but have time to invest in your book, the opportunity cost of using your time to invest in your book is that you reduce the ability to invest that same time in another venture. That other venture could produce a better (R.O.I.) for your time.

Your Definition of Success

We each have our own idea of success. For one writer it could be to have one bestselling book on Amazon, for another it could be to Sell 10,000 copies of their book. Your personal definition can determine your goals.

One book alone may not achieve your goals and if you are continually investing time and money in your book, at some point you need to decide if this is a viable option.

Producing more books or aggressive marketing strategies are just a couple of options to improve the chances of achieving your publishing goals.

Because one option can be more time intensive and another more financially intensive, it is important that you factor your budget into your plans.

Your Author Business

Looking at the millions of books currently selling on Amazon, it is clear that there is a potential market of readers. One book may not make you a fortune but when you start to focus on your writing for its potential earnings, there are undoubtedly some business opportunities.

In one of my previous books "FBA - Building an Amazon Business", I talk about the fact that you can run an Amazon Selling business from anywhere with a laptop and the Internet.

The same can be true for a business built around book publishing but with several advantages:

- When selling books and other digital products (rather than a business that is just selling physical products), you should never run out of stock. Print on demand and digital content mean that there is no longer a necessity for authors to pay for a print run of a thousand books and have them gathering dust in their garage.
- If you want to sell more products (books) on your Amazon account, there is no need to search for manufacturers and negotiate prices. You are the manufacturer and you can have ultimate control over your books.

Case Study

One of the reasons that most people have an idea for a book but it never progresses through to completion, is that they only focus on the writing phase.

In order for you to get the most out of this book, my intention is to provide you with as many tools and aides as possible to cover the whole publishing process.

Working through the exercises below will allow you to take stock of your personal situation.

If you're like me, you find a blank page frustrating and slows you down in formulating solutions.

To help speed things up I've provided you a case study, which you can use as a guide for the exercises.

Case Study George
George is a fifty-year-old business coach who has been successfully coaching individuals for several years. George operates primarily from his home office. He knows that his knowledge and experience could benefit a lot more clients if he condensed his training systems into a book.

George Has a Monthly Income of $10,000 and the same 24 hours in each day, which we all have.

Financial Spending
Below is a breakdown of his financial Spending divided into four categories:

- Household Expenses.
- Business Expenses.
- Savings Allocation.
- Discretionary Spending.

A. Household Expenses

Expense	Amount	Remarks
Monthly Grocery Spend	$1,500	
Monthly Petrol Spend	$800	
Mortgage Payments	$2,000	
Monthly Utilities	$300	
Sub Total	$4,600	

B. Business Expenses

Expense	Amount	Remarks
Business Insurance	$500	
Office Costs	$500	
Accountants Fees	$200	
Lawyers' Fees	$300	
Mobile Phone Plan	$125	
Sub Total	$1,625	

C. Savings Allocation

Expense	Amount	Remarks
Automatic Payment to 401k	$500	
Automatic Payment to savings	$500	
Sub Total	$1,000	

D. Discretionary Spending

Expense	Amount	Remarks
Monthly Cable TV Package	$350	
Monthly Alcohol Spend	$400	
Credit Card Repayment	$350	
Entertainment	$300	
Emergency fund	$500	

Sub Total	$1,900	

E. Overview of allocations

Allocation	Cost	Remarks
Household Expenses	$4,600	
Business Expenses	$1,625	
Savings Allocation	$1,000	
Discretionary Spending	$1,900	
Total Funds allocated	$9,125	
Unallocated Funds	$875	$10,000 - $9,125

By auditing his monthly spending, George has determined that he has $875 a month currently unallocated.

He decides to allocate $500 a month for a period of four months (making a total of $2,000) towards the book project.

Time Monitoring
For the purpose of estimating his time budget, George divides his time up into five categories:

- Work
- Travel
- Eating
- Sleep
- Other

George Tracks the number of fifteen-minute sessions in each day that he spends in each category.

1. Monday

Category	Number of 15 mins Periods	Total Time (mins)	Remarks
Work	36	540	
Travel	8	120	
Eating	8	120	
Sleep	32	480	
Other	12	180	

2. Tuesday

Category	Number of 15 mins Periods	Total Time (mins)	Remarks
Work	36	540	
Travel	8	120	
Eating	8	120	
Sleep	32	480	
Other	12	180	

3. Wednesday

Category	Number of 15 mins Periods	Total Time (mins)	Remarks
Work	36	540	
Travel	8	120	
Eating	8	120	
Sleep	32	480	
Other	12	180	

4. Thursday

Category	Number of 15 mins Periods	Total Time (mins)	Remarks
Work	36	540	
Travel	8	120	
Eating	8	120	
Sleep	32	480	
Other	12	180	

5. Friday

Category	Number of 15 mins Periods	Total Time (mins)	Remarks
Work	36	540	
Travel	8	120	
Eating	8	120	
Sleep	32	480	
Other	12	180	

6. Saturday

Category	Number of 15 mins Periods	Total Time (mins)	Remarks
Work	4	60	
Travel	0	0	
Eating	10	150	
Sleep	36	540	
Other	46	690	

7. Sunday

Category	Number of 15 mins Periods	Total Time (mins)	Remarks
Work	8	120	
Travel	0	0	
Eating	10	150	
Sleep	36	540	
Other	46	630	

8. Total Time allocated to "Other" category

Day	Total Time (mins)	Total Time (hours)	Remarks
Monday	180	3	
Tuesday	180	3	
Wednesday	180	3	
Thursday	180	3	
Friday	180	3	
Saturday	690	11.5	
Sunday	630	10.5	Total 37 hours

When he totals up the amount of time allocated, George finds that he has 37 hours allocated to the "Other" category.

George decides to allocate a minimum of two hours a day (14 hours a week) for four months to the book.

As this still gives him twenty-three hours in reserve each week, he believes this is easily achievable.

Exercises

When you are first starting out as a writer you may have set aside some savings and decided to head off to a log cabin (in the woods) for six months and write your manuscript. Even in this scenario, you will need to dedicate time and money to the publishing process.

For most writers when they are first starting out they are writing alongside their current employment and may not be initially looking at their writing as a business.

It is easy to underestimate the commitment required to publish a book. We all have our own perception of how much time and money we have available but I think it is important that you take stock of this before you can set your budget.

In the following exercises you are going to calculate how much discretionary time and money, you have available to commit to this process.

Exercise One   Financial Spending

In this exercise I want you to determine how much discretionary spending that you have available, to commit to the publishing process.

As most of us now make our payments digitally, it can be relatively easy to review our bank and credit card statements to track our spending.

Here you are going to make a list of where you have previously allocated your income.

Apply the four categories below to each of the items in your list of expenditures:

A. Household Expenses
• Apply this to all of your monthly expenses (utilities, fuel etc.).

- Include your groceries here. If you regularly indulge in luxury items of food or drink, list those items under discretionary spending.

B. Business Expenses
- This may be easy to calculate. If you don't currently run a business it should be zero.

C. Savings
- You may have automated savings coming out of your income.
- As compound interest works best when you start to save early, I am not recommending that you stop contributing to your savings.

D. Discretionary Spending
- This includes any social spending but also any expenses that can be reduced (If an item isn't in one of the other three categories it should be here).
- If you have a mobile phone plan or a cable TV package can you reduce these costs?
- If you have credit card payments can you negotiate reduced payments?

The key here is that the sum total of these four figures should equal the total of all of your income.

People can either underestimate or overestimate the funds that they have available. By actually reviewing our current situation, it allows us to make educated decisions.

Once you have completed this exercise, it is up to you to prioritize what you choose to continue to use your funds for.

Exercise Two   Time Monitoring

For this exercise divide the next seven days into 15-minute segments and log your activities during each of those time-frames.

You can choose to track this in a spreadsheet or in a notebook but I encourage you to update this log as often as possible. There are productivity apps (such as "Focus Keeper") that allow you to set a timer for a 15 minute period. Feel free to use one of these if it helps you.

If you choose to list your activities at the end of each day (rather than regularly updating your log during the day) you may find it hard to remember how much time you devoted to each activity.

Rather than classifying your time into lots of sub-categories I find using the following five categories works best:

1. Work: This relates to any income generating activity.

2. Travel: This relates to travel to and from work so if you work from home this category may be redundant for you.

3. Eating: Although eating food is essential to living a two-hour lunch break is not necessarily the same thing. Therefore, log the time you actually spend eating. For a two-hour lunch, it may be 15 minutes of eating and the rest would be allocated under "other."

4. Sleep: We don't always understand how long we actually sleep so log your hours in bed resting (a midday snooze can also be logged here).

5. Other: I am not suggesting that the first four categories are the only important activities you undertake but sticking with just five categories will make it easier to update your log regularly.

For anything in this category just write a one or two-word answer (such as Facebook, Netflix or date night).

At some time or another, you have probably heard the saying "there are never enough hours in a day." We all have the same 24 hours each day and by working through this exercise, you now have some idea where you allocate yours.

Exercise Three   Commitment

Now that you have determined where you spend your time and money, I want you to make a commitment to yourself.

Over the next twelve months, you need to determine how much you are prepared to commit to the publishing success of your book.

I have chosen twelve months as a benchmark as lots of people set annual goals (so find it easiest to plan for a year). If you have chosen to publish your book in less or more than a twelve month period then adjust your timescale.

As we all have different priorities you need to consider your personal circumstances and what will work for you before making a commitment.

- Financially - look at your discretionary spending budget and decide on a realistic amount to commit. You do not need to create a detailed financial business plan here. Just pick an amount and write it in a statement.

  e.g. "I am making a financial commitment to allocate $25 a week to the budget of my publishing success."

- Time - look at the "Other" category of your available time and decide on a realistic amount to commit. Just pick an amount and write it in a statement.

e.g. "I am making a commitment to allocate one hour every weekday (for the next six months) to the budget of my publishing success".

As I mentioned in the opportunity cost section, you need to balance your time and money expenditure. Once you've made these commitments they aren't set in stone. You can choose to monitor and adjust them as you proceed through the publishing process.

NB.   After reading this chapter you may have already determined that you don't want to commit the time or finances necessary to publish a book. If you do decide to proceed I hope that you now have a more solid foundation to build on.

Chapter 2 Choosing your Niche or Genre

*"You can't be admitted to the ranks of writers of importance unless you have sales." — **James Salter***

One of the key ways to increase your book sales is to make your book visible to the right potential readers.

You may have heard that when you are writing a book you need to determine your niche or genre. You may have also been told it is important to choose the right category when you list your book on Amazon.

Although it is important to start with the end in mind, all of this terminology can seem complicated and confusing.

In reality, all of these terms are just different ways of classifying your book and as we progress through this chapter, these terms will be clarified.

Niches, Types, Genres and Categories
Niches
As your book is a product, you need to determine who the customers are for your product.

When marketers use the term Niche they are referring to a specific section (or group) of society that have similar interests. Due to the common interests in a niche, they tend to gravitate towards similar products or services.

Niche Marketing is about:

A. Identifying a specific group of customers.
B. Identifying the products and services that they favour.
C. Providing those products and services to that group.

An example of a Niche could be the individuals known as "Preppers". Preppers are a section of society that believes a catastrophic disaster is likely to occur in the future, and actively prepare to survive that catastrophe.

There are estimated to be over three million Preppers in the United States alone, which is a reasonable customer base for any niche. Typical types of product that are marketed to preppers are survival supplies and this includes books on survival training etc.

If you only wrote Survival books, it would clearly make sense to target some of your marketing in this niche.

Types
There are primarily two types of books, "Fiction" and "Non-Fiction".

As you would expect, fiction is work created from someone's imagination and non-fiction is based on fact.

There can be some crossover between the two types, but for the purpose of simplification, here we will assume that your book is easily classified as fiction or non-fiction.

Genres
When we split the two types of books into sub-types these can also be referred to as "genres".

- Examples of a non-fiction genres are biographies or memoirs.
- Examples of fiction genres are romance novels or adventure stories.

The genre classifications for books is a way of letting the reader know what to expect from the book. Although the number of genres has grown over time, for as long as we have had books they have been split into genres.

Categories

There are a lot of similarities between the genre of a book and the Amazon category for the same book.

They are both breaking down the types of a book into sub-types but Amazon categories are not just for books, all products on Amazon are divided into categories. The categories in the Amazon store are similar to the aisles in a supermarket and the sub-categories are similar to the shelves in the supermarket.

Consider the "clothing, shoes and jewelry category" on Amazon, it can be broken down into various sub-categories (such as male, female, etc.).

We'll dive deeper into some book sub-categories later in this chapter but for now just be aware, that Amazon has categories to optimize their online storage system.

Category Strings

The term string refers to the continuous line of sub-categories inside sub-categories that your book is listed in.

Just like a Russian doll has more dolls inside the smaller dolls, a string has more sub-categories inside a sub-category.

An example of a category string for a book is:

- Kindle Store > Kindle eBooks > Comics & Graphic Novels > Teen & Young Adult

Your Target audience

Although our book's genre is important to identify our target market, as we are initially aiming at Amazon for most of our book sales, we need to focus on the listing category. Choosing the correct category can be one way of optimizing our chances with the Amazon algorithm.

Algorithm

Throughout this book, you will hear the term "Amazon Algorithm" mentioned several times.

For now just be aware that this is a mathematical calculation that Amazon uses to determine which products are more likely to result in sales to each customer.

The algorithm is fed by multiple pieces of data (including the number of sales of a product and the number of reviews that a product receives). Once it's determined which item customers want, the algorithm tries to show those customers items matching those specific criteria.

Diversifying or specializing

It can be confusing being told to specialize in one niche, type of book or genre when you see some of the successful writers like Joanna Penn, rocking it in non-fiction and several fiction genres. The fact is that they focused on one area, and then when it was established they then added other genres to their portfolio.

I am not suggesting that after you write your first book, if you decide that you hate writing in that genre, that you are stuck with it.

If your initial writing hits some resistance, take two things into account:

- Is it writing in this specific genre that is a problem or writing in general? Only you can determine if this is resistance to the new skill of writing or if the subject matter doesn't suit you.
- To keep you initially focused on mastering one genre before diversifying remember the old adage "The person who chases two rabbits catches none."

Data and the science for sales

One of the ways that you can increase your book sales is through the correct selection of book categories.

Although category selection may produce varied results in fiction or non-fiction there are some commonalities in the approach to both.

In order to provide clarity, I have broken the next part of this chapter into five sections:

1. Know your Audience.
2. Category Choices.
3. Writing to Market.
4. Additional Categories.
5. Paid Tools to Help You.

1. Know your Audience

Books can be classified in various ways but the main thing to know about your book is who your audience is.

Evergreen Audiences

In an ideal world, your book will be popular and continue to sell millions of copies for the rest of your life.

The sales will not dip at any time and the subject matter for your book will never need updating.

In reality, all sales will fluctuate and some books may flop while others are later revived.

Seasonal Audiences

There are certain optimal times for certain books to sell. Some of these are due to specific events, some depend on subjects being in vogue and some relate to certain times of the year.

After the 2016 American Elections, lots of books came out in the area of politics because it was a profitable area for books.

Each year around the Christmas Holidays Self Help / Personal development books are targeted at the large group of people resolving to make the next year better.

In recent years a twist on a classic tale has been popular in fiction. "Abraham Lincoln Vampire Slayer" is just one story that comes to mind. This might work for a Hollywood blockbuster but for books it is easier to tap into current markets than try to create your own.

Popular Audiences

When we look at popular genres such as romance, they have voracious readers that are continually looking for content. If there are lots of readers, it probably means that there are lots of established authors in those genres.

Competition is not necessary a bad thing as it means that there is definitely an audience for your genre of book.

All famous authors start somewhere and it is a lot easier to produce a product for a waiting market, than to try and create a market for your product.

2. Category Choices

With all of the different sub-categories, it can be difficult to determine where to list your books.

As I said earlier, we are aiming to sell our book on Amazon, although readers may not search by category we want to ensure that our book is grouped with similar books.

When I was recently starting my own fiction series, I chose to look at similar books in order to define my genre.

The series is a futuristic Science fiction Fantasy that contains aspects of several classic stories. I decided to look for five to ten books in the same ballpark as my books.

As the setting is a futuristic Dystopia I initially looked at "The Hunger Games". When I clicked on the book on Amazon it also displayed (in the section "customers who bought this item also bought") "Divergent" and "The Maze Runner".

The Hunger Games Kindle Store Category String:

- Kindle Store > Kindle eBooks > Comics & Graphic Novels > Teen & Young Adult

Divergent Kindle Category String:

- Kindle Store > Kindle eBooks > Teen & Young Adult > Science Fiction & Fantasy > Science Fiction > Dystopian

The Maze Runner Kindle Store Category String:

- Kindle Store > Kindle eBooks > Teen & Young Adult > Science Fiction & Fantasy > Science Fiction > Action & Adventure

One of the key elements of my series is the way the poor are fed and so I gravitated towards the film "Soylent Green".
Make Room, Make room (This book is the basis for the film Soylent green) Kindle Store Category Strings:

- Kindle Store > Kindle eBooks > Science Fiction & Fantasy > Science Fiction > Classics
- Kindle Store > Kindle eBooks > Science Fiction & Fantasy > Fantasy

My series has an aspect of the downtrodden being controlled by misinformation and fighting against a better equipped evil organization so I looked to Star Wars and 1984.

Star wars Kindle Store Category Strings:

- Kindle   Store > Kindle   eBooks > Science   Fiction   & Fantasy > Science   Fiction > TV,   Movie,   Video   Game Adaptations > Star Wars
- Kindle Store > Kindle eBooks > Literature & Fiction > Action & Adventure > Fantasy

1984 Category Strings:

- Kindle   Store > Kindle   eBooks > Science   Fiction   & Fantasy > Science Fiction > Classics
- Kindle   Store > Kindle   eBooks > Literature   & Fiction > Classics > Literary

As you can see from the details of the listings above most of the books share commonalities in the Science Fiction & Fantasy Sub Genre. Some of the Books are aimed at Teen and Young adults but others are more literature based so where is my target audience here?

Drilling down to Sub-category
For My book I picked the main genre of Science fiction and then asked the following questions:

a) What is the age of my target audience? (As my main characters were teens to twenty-something in age), I spanned Young Adult/Millennials.
b) Are there any supernatural beings in my storylines (Aliens, Werewolves etc.)?
c) What elements make my story stand out?

3. Additional Categories

Once you your book listed under the initial two categories (that Amazon offers you) there is the opportunity to gain more exposure by listing your book under additional categories.

You can list in these extra categories by simply contacting Amazon and asking for your book to be added. (It is suggested that you start by asking to be added to one extra category at a time).

Although not all readers search on Amazon by book category it makes sense to give your book as much visibility as possible.

As an example of searching by category, I have just typed in "Vampires" into the book search on Amazon and one of the books that came up was listed under:

- Kindle ebooks > Romance
- Kindle ebooks >Science Fiction & Fantasy

As you can see they are two different strings and as lots of books span several categories, you want to give your book the highest visibility.

Be aware that trying to list a cowboy book in the same category as "Dungeons and Dragons" type books may annoy readers and be counterproductive.

The process for asking for your book to be listed in extra categories is relatively simple:

When you contact Amazon you need to give them your book's title (include sub titles), the ASIN of your book and the full category string that you want your book to be listed under.

In order to add a category you need to Login to the author Central Home Page (We'll be covering "Author Central" later in the book so feel free to come back here later).

The process (as listed on Amazon's help section) is:

- Click on the "Contact Us" button (currently a big yellow button at the top left of the screen).
- When the "Contact Us" form pops up you need to choose the following selections from the drop down menus (in Section 1):
  - Under "Select an issue," select "MY BOOKS"
  - Under "Select details," select "UPDATE INFORMATION ABOUT A BOOK"
  - Select "BROWSE CATEGORIES"
  - Select "I WANT TO UPDATE MY BOOK'S BROWSE CATEGORIES"
- In section 2, you will be given the option "HOW WOULD YOU LIKE TO CONTACT US"
  - E-MAIL
  - PHONE
- When you click on the circle next to email section 3 opens up and you can just type your information into the space under "QUESTION/FEEDBACK" and click "SUBMIT"

An example of a request is:

I'd like my book, (Gratitude for Happiness: How to exercise your gratitude muscles) with ASIN number (B073RYS4CB) to be added to the following category: (Kindle Store > Kindle eBooks > Nonfiction > Self-Help > spiritual)

4. Writing to Market

Although you might want to choose your writing genre based on the size of the market and profitability, your creative writing ability and your passion will probably be the main drivers of your choice of writing genre.

Most fiction genres are well serviced (they have lots of books and authors) and this means that they provide both competition and a potential market.

Certain Authors such as Stephen King have dominated a genre by their sheer volume of works and if that is your long-term goal then your choice of a genre may be as mathematical as it is creative.

Choosing one genre and sticking to it (initially) is a great way of building your brand.

You may believe that you only have one book in you but as the odds against one book providing you an income are high, you should consider your long-term goals.

Sizing up the Competition

The first step in this outline is choosing your niche.

When reviewing niches you need to set a benchmark to determine how successful the books in that niche are currently doing.

I look at the top five books and ask the following questions?

A. Is this niche dominated by international stars in their field? E.g. if I was writing a self-help book am I competing against the likes of Brian Tracy, Anthony Robbins, Brendon Bouchard etc.

B. How many reviews have the top sellers in this niche got (just choose the top five books and check the review count)? If the top books have been published for over 3 months and have less than 50 reviews, this may not be a profitable niche.

C. How much are these books making a month? You can look at their Amazon bestseller ranking to get a rough estimate of the book sales. By focusing on the overall Amazon bestseller ranking rather than the ranking in that niche you won't get dragged into a dying niche.

Ideally, you want to see that the top ten books BSRs are below 30,000.

There is also software available that will analyze this information on Amazon for you (this is usually purchased as a browser add-on), such as Jungle Scout etc.

D. How many books are there already in this field? You actually want a niche that has lots of books rather than fewer books as this is a market that you can tap into.

E. How good are the current book listings in your niche? It won't surprise you to know that marketing can make the difference in your sales.

- Can you write a better book description (using HTML and good copywriting can make an average book stand out over a better book)?
- Can you produce a better book cover (see the chapter on book covers)?
- Can you produce a more up to date version on the subject matter (just having something like "2018 edition on your book cover can make it stand out)?

5. Paid Tools to Help You

Indie authors can become obsessed with reducing financial spending on their book.

Although I don't believe in paying for too many tools initially, data analysis can save you hours of manual research.

I have laid out some of the manual techniques above but if you are serious about optimizing your book sales, I highly recommend using a data analysis tool.

At the time of writing this book, there are several tools on the market (such as K-Lytics, KDP Rocket or Kindle Spy) that can provide data to help you determine profitable genres and how to optimize publishing in certain niches.

These tools provide reports on categories, sub-categories etc. and can be a useful tool as you proceed on your publishing journey.

If you do have limited funds for a data analysis tool, a one-off payment may be more cost-effective than paying monthly subscriptions. At the time of writing this book, KDP Rocket has a one-off payment model.

I will provide a list of current tools in the resources appendix of this book, but I encourage you to spend a little time finding the one that is the best fit for you.

Exercises

The main focus of this chapter has been to identify where your readers are. Getting your book in front of the right readers is one of the keys to selling your books.

Exercise Four   Identifying Your Category

This exercise is geared at a manual strategy but if you choose to use a data analysis tool such as KDP Rocket, use that technique to choose your category faster.

- Search Amazon for the ten books that are closest to your book.
- Write down the categories and sub-categories of these books.
- Choose the two most common category strings.

- Note these categories for your future listing.

Remember that you may add further category strings after your book is live so take a note of the other category strings of the ten books.

If you can't find two common category strings from the first ten books you choose, keep searching similar books until you find them.

Exercise Five   Identifying the Top Books in Your Category

As you are starting on this writing journey you want to get the feel for the other books in the categories that you are writing.

Typing in a term such as "top 100 romance Novels" in Amazon's bookstore may give you varied results.

The Amazon Algorithm works on real-time data so the top 100 today may not be the top 100 tomorrow (if a new book suddenly has lots of sales).

For accurate data, I highly recommend purchasing or subscribing to analytical software but initially I just want you to get a feel for your competition.

In the Amazon Search box, choose kindle store from the drop-down menu and type in the box:

- Top 100 (insert your genre) books. If your book doesn't fall under an obvious genre (such as "Western Books" or "Romance") you may have to try a few different search terms.

You are going to look at the covers, titles and book descriptions in order to get a feel for those books before you proceed through this book.

As your search attempts can give you a variety of results I want you to use the following criteria to classify the books as your top five:

- The books with the highest number of reviews.
- The books with the lowest BSR (Best Seller Ranking).
- The books with the highest star rating for their reviews.

- The books that have a publication date within the last six months.

Although this criteria isn't all-encompassing it will give you an idea of what books are succeeding. Just pick the top two or three books and see if they are books that you would like to buy.

Chapter 3 Launch Schedules

"Nothing is particularly hard if you divide it into small jobs." —
Henry Ford

The word "schedule" is defined as "a plan for carrying out a process or procedure".

It might seem odd to talk about the launch schedule for your book, if you haven't even started writing your content yet. There are a lot of activities for your book launch that I class as "Seed Activities".

A seed activity is something that you need to start in advance for it to produce results (bear fruit) when you need those results. If you don't plant those seeds in advance it's going to be a very lean harvest!

By considering your launch now, you are starting with your end goals in mind and giving yourself a better chance of a successful book launch.

In this chapter, you will find activities that you can start immediately and information on activities that you can schedule for later.

Once you get immersed in your writing time can pass quickly, so I implore you to start now with a plan for your launch schedule.

1. Your Email List
If you have ever heard anyone promoting email lists for marketing purposes, you have no doubt heard the phrase "The Sooner you start building your email list the better!"

If we look at just one successful author (and online Entrepreneur) Pat Flynn. Pat has over 88,000 subscribers to his Youtube channel, over 153,000 followers on Twitter, over 35,000 followers on Instagram and over 34,000 members in his Facebook group.

I think you will agree that he is no slouch when it comes to building a social media presence, yet he states that one of his biggest regrets was not building his email list earlier.

If you intend to lock yourself away in a monastery for ten years (with no interactions with the outside world) to write your masterpiece, then you may want to outsource your list building. If you are not heading off into social oblivion then you can start to build your list now.

There are a multitude of courses and books focused solely on list building and I have suggested some of those resources in the appendix at the end of this book.

Although I won't be covering the whole process to build your email list here, I have provided a few tips below:

- Determine Your Niche — Determining your niche needs to be one of your first steps as you want to ensure that the people on your email list match your content. The content you provide is meant to serve the recipients and the core question they are asking (when they receive your email) is "What's in it for me?"
- Your Emails Are Going to Real People — It may seem like it is just a numbers game. Realizing that only a certain percentage of your email list opens your emails and only a certain percentage of those accepts the included offers, it can seem like your subscribers are just statistics. Remember that your subscribers are real people and it is your responsibility to keep them engaged with quality content.
- Do Not Abuse Subscribers Trust — Some unscrupulous people have been known to share their email list with other people.

When a subscriber gave you their email they did so because they trusted you, do not break that trust. You will not get that trust back.

- Keep The Content Relevant to Each List — If you publish in more than one genre, you should have separate email lists for each genre. Automated systems (such as autoresponders) allow you to build separate lists and by categorizing them it will avoid confusion. Sending information on Dystopian Zombie Books to readers of Romance Novels is one example of the wrong content for the wrong market.

- You Don't Need an Expensive Website — There can be so much to learn and so many potential expenses when you are first starting out as an Indie. Luckily companies such as Convertkit.com provide tools and resources (such as Landing Pages) at minimal cost to get you started. You can build your website later but as you don't need a website to start your list, there is no excuse not to start building your list now.

- Have An Alternative Address — When you input your details into a form or Landing page, by law you must a physical address. If you don't want your home address to go out at the bottom of every email you will need to have an alternative or business address ready when you start this process.

- Target Readers in Your Niche — Running a competition to win the top five books in your niche (And promoting the competition through Facebook Ads, etc.) can help fill your list with the right readers. Promoting your competition to the authors of those books can help give you exposure to their lists.

N.B. Most people avoid building a list because they think they have nothing to offer subscribers. Don't fall into this trap. If you wait until you have a completed manuscript before you start on your list, you will still need content for your subscribers, to market your book.

2. Build Relationships with Social Media

When you are first starting out with your writing, you may have only a limited (or no) presence on Social Media.

Most people have a Facebook account and that can be your first Segue into Facebook groups and other social media platforms.

I'll assume that you have already got a Facebook account (if not go set one up now), start out by joining three Facebook groups that seem relevant to your book.

It may be easier for a fiction writer to find a Facebook group such as "Marketing for Romance Writers" (or other groups relevant to your genre) than a group dedicated to Non-Fiction writers. If you can't find a suitable genre look at groups such as "Indie Authors" or "Self-publishing".

Social currency

Building relationships on social Media requires building social currency (goodwill), more "Seed Activities". Once you've joined these groups allocate some time each day to engage in these groups, comment on other people's posts (respectfully) and start to be seen as useful. Most of these groups are full of helpful people so ask questions to help increase your knowledge.

Ensure that you stick to the rules of the group!

Other Social Platforms

There are lots of options to promote and market on social media but to get the most benefits you need to establish yourself as a contributor rather than join a network and just start marketing yourself.

Depending on your budget you might want to hire someone to help you build a presence on various platforms. It can be time-consuming posting on all the different social platforms (even with automation and scheduling).

If you are going to do all of the marketing yourself, initially start with one platform e.g. Facebook or Twitter and master that platform.

For Twitter, Instagram, Pinterest etc. it is recommended that you share other people's content initially. A ratio of sharing 70-80% of other people's content and making up the balance with your own content can be a good way of getting noticed.

Rather than sharing blindly, focus on two or three influencers in your niche or genre, initially follow them and share their content.

3. Build a Launch Team

You may have heard the terms Beta Readers, Street Team or Launch Team. This is a group of individuals that support you and provide feedback on your work.

Wouldn't it be great to have readers that provide you feedback before you publish? Imagine if those same readers are ready to review the book in the first week of listing, rather than launching your book off into the void?

Your team can come from your email list, social media list or anyone you choose.

- Tracking them through a spreadsheet can be useful but opening a separate Facebook group can centralize all of your information in one place.
- Be specific on what feedback you require, to keep your launch timetable on schedule. This group is not designed to replace an editor.

- Too much feedback can be distracting and (in the early stages of your writing career) has the potential to damage your confidence.

Choose this team wisely but above all seek them out early.

4. Content Creation isn't Publishing

When you first start writing you may think that the time spent producing content for your book is the most important period of your publishing journey.

Although I am paraphrasing here, there is a saying that "once you have your book 90% completed, that you are half way there". It is important to realize early on that writing a book is similar to creating any product, in that manufacturing is only part of the sales process.

Although this book is focused on the Kindle version of your book, if you intend to have the book available in different formats from the offset you need to take that into account for your launch schedule. One of the first reviews (that I received for my first book) was a four-star review, it stated that they would have given it a five-star review but there was no paperback available at the time of the launch.

If you are launching a book at $0.99 for the digital version, you may get some paperback sales early. Even if you are not focused on early paperback sales, having extra formats of your book available give your book more credibility.

5. The Date of Your Launch is Not Your Publication Date

Some publishing terminology can be incorrectly used (or understood). To ensure that we are on the same page I want to state from the outset that "Your book launch is not the day that your book listing goes live on Amazon!" The day your book is available for sale (goes live) is a component of the launch process but not the whole launch.

If you are anything like me, when you are publishing your first book you will be impatient. Although the publication of my first book was a bit of an accident, even I was eager to get it live on Amazon.

Most authors see publishing their first book as the culmination of years of commitment and all that built up excitement can mean a rush to go live.

You need to approach your book launch tactically. Most of us are familiar with the type of product launch that the Apple Corporation has perfected over the years.

I think you'll agree that having people sleep outside stores in preparation for the launch of new Apple products, hasn't come about by secretly stocking the product on shelves and waiting for customers to discover them.

Although that (idea of just letting customers discover new Apple products) might be a cool marketing idea now that they are established, in reality, product launches require a schedule and an organized plan.

You may remember one of the first sentences in this book stated that "Your book is a product." You should focus on your book launch as a product launch.

6. Your Books First Thirty Days
The first thirty days of your Amazon's book listing are key to a successful launch.

When your book first goes live on Amazon it starts an unofficial countdown period of around thirty days. This period is not listed anywhere on Amazon but it is widely accepted by Amazon sellers.

This initial launch period is often referred to in forums as the honeymoon period. Basically, when you first start selling your book on Amazon, it is given an initial chance to get established by the Amazon algorithm.

The Amazon Algorithm and the Technical Stuff
I mentioned previously that the Amazon algorithm is a mathematical formula that combines various pieces of sales data. The Algorithm analyses the data of your book to give it a BSR (Best Seller Ranking).

As we learned in the last chapter, the numerous categories on Amazon are just like the departments or aisles in any store. From Laundry Detergent and Diapers to Books, every item, in every category on Amazon has a BSR.

During this initial period your books BSR will start off low but if you don't start to sell books, the algorithm will start to penalize you and give you a higher ranking. You are in effect accruing penalty points.

Why a Lower Seller Ranking Is Better Than a Higher One
Terms such as Algorithm and Seller Ranking can seem very technical to first-time authors but the basic premise is that the more sales and success your book gathers, the lower the ranking your book will be allocated.

Visualize your book's seller ranking like the position in any other competition.

First place receives a better prize than third place, hence it is better to be ranked with the lower number one (or first) than the higher number three (or third).

Amazon gives preferential treatment to products with a lower BSR by making them more visible in search results. Now you start to see why you should view your book as a product!

30 Days Is Not the Whole Life of Your Book
You may hear long-term marketing strategists arguing that authors focus too much on the first 30 days of their books life.

Although you need to have a long-term strategy for your book marketing, it is important to give it a good start in life.

As long-term planning can seem a bit overwhelming for new authors, it can also provide a psychological boost to achieve some success in this shorter timeframe.

7. Pre-orders
Because of the importance of the first thirty days, Pre-orders can be a good way of priming your initial sales pump.

The term Pre-Order refers to the fact that customers can order a product in advance of it being available for sale. When setting up your book for sale on Amazon KDP, you have the option to make it available for sale immediately or make it available for Pre-order.

Although customers can't download samples (or receive the book on their Kindle) during the Pre-order period, Amazon will show your book's listing page on their platform.

Timing
The Pre-order process allows customers to order your book up to ninety days before its release date.

Your draft manuscript must go through the Amazon review process to confirm that it complies with their policies. Once your draft is approved you may make changes but these will also need to be reviewed.

To ensure that your book has time for review and approval before the release date there is a deadline for submitting the final manuscript. Amazon conveniently provides you a countdown timer on that book titles setup pages, to keep track of the upcoming submission deadline.

8. Advanced Review Copies (ARCs)

Distribution of ARCs before a book launch has been one of the recognized methods of book promotion since traditional publishing first begun.

Formats for ARCs

When Publishers initially sent out ARCs they were probably unbound printed copies of the books. In today's digital universe, ARCs are more likely to be distributed as PDF's or Mobi files.

PDF (Portable Document Format) Files are used rather than other documents such as MS Word Documents because they are less easy to edit. Mobi (a form of the documents known as Epub) files are a digital format that Amazons Kindle e-reader uses.

PDF's and mobi files can be emailed to your Kindles email address, thus adding them to your Kindle's Library. The issue is that when you try to read the two formats on your Kindle, they behave differently. A PDF doesn't have the same functionality so it makes the reading experience inferior.

Because you are publishing your book on Kindle, you want Kindle readers to get the best experience when reading your ARC, so have a Mobi version of your book available. Although there are free online converters (that convert PDF files to Mobi files), the converted layout is not the same as the PDF.

One of the easiest ways to create a Mobi file is to download a copy from KDP during the online review process. I cover this in more detail in the section on "Kindle eBook Previewer" in chapter four.

Concerns about file security
One of the biggest fears that Indie authors voice is that they are worried about the security of their digital files.

Counterfeiting is not a new problem for Artists, from the forgery of masterpieces (such as the Mona Lisa) to cassette tapes recording songs off vinyl records and radio shows, our work will never be 100% secure.

If we go back to the fact that your book is a product and then consider that the latest Calloway Golf Driver can be reverse engineered (and counterfeited) within days of its release, you would wonder why people manufacture at all.

Shortly after I published my first book a friend of mine asked if I would Skype his brother in India and discuss the subject matter. I asked if his brother needed a copy of the book and was told that my friend had bought a Kindle copy on Amazon and created a copy of this (and sent it to him). I was initially unhappy that my friend had counterfeited my book and scolded him. The main lesson I took away from this incident, was that once you have launched your book, the genie is out of the bottle and can never be put back.

Of course, you should pursue copyright infringements on your work, but don't let fear of counterfeiting stop you distributing ARC copies of your book.

Copyrighting
The Term Copyright refers to your legal ownership rights to an original work that you have created. Although copyright laws differ slightly in different countries, there are some international

agreements (such as the Bernie Convention) that provide some standard rules for Copyright.

Copyright doesn't just refer to written works, music or even cartoon characters (such as Micky Mouse) can be copyrighted. As an author, you do not have to register your work to own its Copyright (in countries adhering to international rules) you are automatically granted the copyrights to your work when it is fixed.

As your success grows and we develop more and more ways of distributing information you may have to deal with infringement of your copyright. If you have had an unpublished manuscript sitting in your desk drawer for years, it may be hard to prove when you produced that work. Publishing your book on Amazon provides a digital record of when your book content was fixed and gives you some evidence should you have to enforce your copyrights.

As digital formats of work are constantly changing and with them legislation, I would suggest that you keep abreast with any changes to the international laws but do not overly worry about copyright when publishing your first book (unless you are plagiarizing someone else's work).

As your portfolio grows remember that your work is classed as Intellectual Property and can be an asset to be passed on to your estate.

9. It's your schedule

You can use Calendars, Project management tools or even a simple table to schedule out your launch. Ideally work with a medium that you are comfortable using, as you will be absorbing enough new information during this process, without adding additional stress.

The fact is that although the choice and testing of some key elements will take time, you need some idea of the launch schedule that you are working towards. Remember it's your schedule so you can always modify this later.

A few of the main launch elements for you to keep in mind are:

- Your scheduled launch date – Set your launch date and work backward to today.
- The scheduled date for all activities – You can adjust your timetable as you go but initially laying out your schedule will help you track your progress.
- Milestones – You need to have a way of confirming that your plan is on track.
- A point of no return – Although you are in charge of the launch schedule, certain elements of the launch (such as online promotion services) have notice requirements. These issues will not stop the launch but can minimize its impact if not rescheduled in time.
- Planning a book launch or Amazon giveaway has to be done in advance. Even sites that promote your giveaways for free require notice (sometimes up to two weeks in advance). They also have lots of books being submitted for their promotion so getting in early makes sense.
- Some sites stipulate you must have at least five reviews before they will promote your book (so getting some prelaunch copies out can help gain some early reviews).

10. Soft Launches
Also known as a pre-launch. The first couple of weeks that your book is live is sometimes referred to as the soft launch.

If you are very efficient at publishing and begin writing a book a week, it doesn't mean you will be launching a book a week.

Certain checks and balances are necessary before a launch. You need to ensure that a book is available and there are no issues with downloads, etc. before you promote that book to a large audience.

What Can a Kindle soft launch include?

- Ensuring that the book is edited and uploaded.
- Ensuring that the book cover is ready and uploaded.
- Generating initial reviews (at least 10 reviews before the proper launch).
- Scheduling the giveaway or countdown deal, your book needs to be live before you can schedule this.
- Scheduling the promotion of your giveaway/countdown deal on as many promotion sites as possible.
- Setting the initial list price of the book.

Extra Options for your Soft launch

- Ensuring that at least one other format (paperback etc.) is ready and uploaded

11. The Full launch

A Full Launch will span all the activities in a Soft Launch but will also include the follow-on activities.

- Ensuring that the promotion is given maximum exposure.
- Updating the list price of the book throughout the various stages.
- Planning your launch ads for the end of the promotion.
- Following up readers for Reviews.
- Further marketing (including social media).

Extra Options for your Full launch

- Ensuring that the digital, print and audio versions of this book are available for the launch?

12. Thinking Outside the box

I am fortunate to remember when Stephen King first launched "The Green Mile," he wanted to publish his book in a series (a bit like the stories in the Old Wild West).

He split the book into six parts, I think the first two parts were launched together and then we had to wait a few weeks for each of the subsequent parts of the book.

He was still writing the book when he published the first two segments so even he didn't know the ending. This strategy created anticipation and like most of the readers, I couldn't wait for each segment of the book to be released. I would equate it to waiting for a weekly episode of Game of Thrones (or some other TV Series) today.

Although this Novel marketing strategy may not have been as successful if Stephen King hadn't been such a well-established author, it shows that adopting novel strategies shouldn't be discounted straight away.

Exercises

Reading this chapter has hopefully impressed on you the need for planning your book in advance. Setting a target in the distance is not necessarily a commitment to achieve a specific deadline. By setting a flexible schedule it can help you avoid procrastination and turn your publishing dream into reality.

Below are a few exercises to help get you started on your publishing journey. Before you dive into the weeds of content creation, please work through these exercises.

Exercise Six   Layout a Basic Launch Schedule

Plan out a basic Launch schedule for your first book. Use the table in Appendix C as your starting point or lay the schedule out using whatever format you are comfortable with. Remember to set your launch date and work backward.

Ensure that you include all of the elements of your book launch such as:

- The publication schedule
- Book editing
- The launch team
- Book cover
- etc etc.

Exercise Seven   Start to Build Your Email List Today

Start to build your email list (Ideally aim to have several hundred people on your list before you launch your book).

1. Choose an autoresponder provider such as:
- "Convertkit"
- "Mailerlite"
- "Mailchimp"

2. Choose a course or resource to guide you through the process of building your email list.

Some examples are:

- Pat Flynn
     https://www.smartpassiveincome.com/email-list-strategies/
- Ryan Levesque   https://www.askmethod.com/
- Nathalie Lussier   https://nathalielussier.com/

If you aren't comfortable with any of the resources listed above, just type "How to build an email list" in a google search and you will find a multitude of options.

Don't delay, pick a resource that you feel comfortable with and begin to build your list

There is no shortage of opportunities to help you build your list and if the voice in your head is telling you, "it's too soon to build a list", it's a liar!

THE KEY ELEMENTS FOR (INDIE) AUTHOR SUCCESS

Chapter 4 The Book Content, Research, and Editing

"Every book you pick up has its own lessons, and quite often the bad books have more to teach than the good ones." — **Stephen King**

One thing that is the same for all books of all genres, you need quality content. Just as a bad ingredient in a meal can be poisonous, if your book content is not of sufficient quality it will ruin your book.

A lot of successful authors look back on their earlier works and despair at the low quality. This doesn't mean that these authors published sub-standard books, it just means that they have improved through time and produced superior work.

Although this chapter is primarily about the content you put in your book, I have added a section based on the Layout of the KDP Platforms "eBook Content Editing" tab.

For first-time Authors working, uploading and updating in the KDP system, can be a scary activity. I have provided some guidelines and information to demystify the KDP system (and to hopefully give you a bit of a confidence boost).

Layout

As most of the elements covered in this book can cross the fiction/non-fiction barrier, when I refer to layout it is concerning the general layout of a book. There are lots of different ways for fiction writers to arrange their stories and numerous creative writing and coaching services for fiction writers. As with all of the content in this book we are discussing elements that you can focus on to optimize your book's success.

Although I appreciate that first drafts can be messy productions, my personal view is if you have laid out your initial content well, it will save you lots of time in the editing phase of your writing process.

Intros and samples

For Non-Fiction Books you may start with an Intro Section and for Fiction, you may include a prologue. Even if you jump straight into a book with your first chapter or poem, the initial impression sets the tone for your book.

The first 10% of your book content is what the reader will see from a sample kindle download. The "Look inside" Feature on Amazon's platform also previews the initial content of your book. If your book doesn't hook a reader from the start you have probably lost them. However good your content is, ensure you start with your best work.

In one of my books, I placed a discreet link to a free course in the book introduction. Because the book introduction shows in Amazon's "Look Inside" feature, I sometimes get sign-ups for the course when people see the link (even if they don't download a sample or buy the book). I see this as an opportunity to provide extra value to potential readers but it is also a way of getting extra exposure at no extra cost.

As I stated in the introduction to this book, all of the elements of your book are related to marketing so always be considering what activities can increase your profile with prospective readers.

Table of Contents

I understand that not all fiction writers include a table of contents but for most writers that do, you should optimize its benefits.

The beauty of an eBook is that the reader can use the links in the Table of Contents (TOC) to quickly navigate the book. There is a balancing act between the ability for a reader to jump to any location in the book and the usefulness of a table of contents.

Ensure that your contents page(s) allows searchability within the book, without taking up too much space. If your TOC has too many sub-headings the reader now has to navigate the TOC, which negates its function.

If that sounds a bit complicated here's the basics:

- When you format your headings and subheadings (in word processing software, such as MS Word) you may use format settings "Heading 1" for the chapter titles, "Heading 2" for the section headings and "Heading 3" for sub-section headings.
- When you create your Table of Contents you can choose to have it include links to just the Heading 1 Text or include links for Heading 2 & Heading 3.
- Each link has a line in the table of contents so it can allow you to go to that specific part of your book (e.g. a line may say "Chapter 1" and be linked to the title at the start of chapter 1).
- If you have lots of section and subsection headings in your book that's a lot of lines in the table of contents.
- A TOC of 1-1.5 pages allows you to scan the table and quickly jump straight to chapter or section of a book.
- If you put too many lines in your TOC and it ends up being 4 or more pages, you now have to search through those pages in order to find a specific line to get to a specific place in the book.

The crux of the matter is that you want the reader to have a pleasant experience when reading your book, a concise table of contents is GOOD, a table of contents that is too long is BAD!

How are You Going to Write Your Book?

Although some authors swear by Scrivener and others are happy with a word processor (such as Microsoft Word), the main thing is to work with what you are comfortable with.

Scrivener is a useful tool for laying out and manipulating the content of your book but for a single non-fiction book, you may just need text documents and a spreadsheet for tracking.

Remember that content creation and editing are two different phases of the publishing process.

There are two trains of thought as to whether to edit as you go or to undertake a larger edit at the end.

Whichever method suits you, the main thing is to have a process in place and create quality content.

Templates

If you are staying in the same niches (or genres) while you create content for your first book you can use the same layout or template for the next book. Having previous templates and processes that you can adapt to future books will speed up the whole process and provide continuity in your writing style.

I am not talking about writing almost the same book under different titles just using the commonalities in books that you will find relevant e.g.

- Disclaimers: Mostly the same wording that you can cut and paste.
- Glossary: Although the content here will be different, the layout such as the alphabet headings will stay the same.
- Act Structure: In a programme such as Scrivener you can duplicate elements of a project rather than trying to create something from scratch.

- Author Pages: Having an up to date author page (with links to your website and other works), is one less thing to prepare in your editing phase.

Research

There may be some crossovers in the subject matter of certain books, so keep all research from previous books (but review it to confirm suitability before adding to a new book).

Having a system for your research can also speed things up for your future books whilst maintaining content quality.

Like most processes, the more often that you work through them, the more efficient you will become.

General Resources

There will be certain information that you add to a book to enhance the reader's value. To save time for future books have this information in a reusable format

- Quotes Bank
  - A lot of the non-fiction gurus have quotes relevant to different niches.
  - Having these quotes in a spreadsheet that allows you to search by subject, and author can save time for future books
  - Having them in the right format (fonts, italics, hyphens between orator and quote etc) can also save time with cutting and pasting
- Recommended authors for Non-Fiction
  - As with a glossary, you will find the layout for recommended authors can be transferrable between books.
  - Having a list of authors, their books, and a quick synopsis can also help save time with future books.

- o If you are writing in the same niche a lot of the same authors may be relevant to more than one of your books.
- Don't just add content
  - o It is often said that the quality of a book is not about what is included in a book but what is left out.
  - o You may have read that a novella should be 17,500-40,000 words or that a Sci-Fi novel should be at least 90,000 words. If you add lots of word content to your manuscript, just to reach a prescribed word count, most of it may be lost in the edit.
  - o Another proverb amongst writers is that "when your book is 90% written you are almost half of the way there". The editing phase of a book can feel brutal for an author, especially if you are removing large sections of text so try to avoid initial padding.

Types of Editing

Traditionally Editing has been broken down into four separate types. You may not require all of these types of editing for your book, but it is important that you know the differences:

- Development Editing

This is what I would call a deep dive or collaboration edit. Some of the activities may be as complex as developing a manuscript from a vague concept to researching and rewriting concept. If you are self-publishing a complex Non-fiction book, you may need to hire someone in this area of expertise.

- Substantive Editing

This kind of editing is designed to improve the flow of a manuscript. For fiction, you may want an editor who is experienced in your genre and for complex Non-fiction someone with the technical abilities to understand the content. Remember that the target audience for your book may be specialized so the content may not be understandable by the average reader.

- Copy Editing

This is what I would refer to as the tidy upstage of the manuscript. The editor is looking for inconsistencies in format, layout, spacing's etc. A copy editor reviews your writing to look for inconsistencies and the general readability of the book. Their tasks can include cross-checking tables, references etc.

- Proofreading

This is the final stage of the Editing process. A proofreader is reading your work with a fresh set of eyes and is looking for any obvious errors and discrepancies. A proofreader may not necessarily be seen as a technical editor but is someone that has a good eye for grammar and is looking for all of those minor issues that may have been missed throughout the rest of the process.

Planning your editing

I understand that some new authors have a limited budget and hiring an Editor may not be part of your plan but you need to ensure that your work is checked by someone else prior to publishing.

Here's a few suggestions to reduce your costs for editing:

- Use a Text to speech Reader for your initial proofread - When you are reading your own work aloud, you can inadvertently miss the odd punctuation mark. By running your test through software that actually reads your words out loud it can make it easier for you to hear issues. There are lots of free tools out there such as "NaturalReaders.com" or MS Words built-in "Speak" function.
  It may sound like a robot is reading your book but if you have missed a comma or full stop (period), the robot will just continue

to read the text. It is amazing how useful this process is for reducing extremely long sentences.

- Find an Editor through a group or network - If you are a member of one or more writers groups (Facebook or otherwise), you will usually find several more experienced writers willing to help out. You may still have to pay them for their time but they can be a lot cheaper than hiring a professional.

Whatever method you choose for your editing ensure that you allow enough time. Whether you are self-editing or hiring someone, producing a polished book can usually take more time than you expect.

NB   Now that you know the different types of editing, check exactly what you are getting when you hire someone. Some authors hire a development editor and then wonder why the book is not ready to upload after just this edit.

Submission

When you have your edited manuscript ready for publication, it can be an emotional time.

This can manifest in various ends of the spectrum, from writers who are glad to finish their work and just want to get published, to perfectionists/procrastinators, who will never believe it's ready.

Below are a few suggestions that should help you work through those emotions and bring you closer to the middle of the spectrum:

- Ensure that you have had at least one person proofread your manuscript before upload.
  - This doesn't have to be a professional editor or even someone that is interested in the subject matter.

- o The main focus here is to get a different set of eyes on your work to look for errors that are glaringly obvious to a layman.
- Check it again
  - o Once you have uploaded your final manuscript and have run it through the digital proofreader, leave it (for at least) a few hours and then check it through again. A read through with a set of fresh eyes makes it easier to spot obvious mistakes.
- Avoid procrastination
  - o Set the number of times that you will review your manuscript before you press submit (and allow KDP to let the book go live), once you have reached that number be prepared to let it go.
  - o If you decided that you would only review the book three times and it still has major errors, then your review process needs some work.
- Nobody's perfect.
  - o As an avid reader, I can state categorically that I have found minor mistakes in multiple bestsellers. Even the likes of Tim Ferris has released books that had initial formatting or spelling mistakes.
  - o I had the word Disclaimer in one of my print books missing the "C" for 12 months (and that was one of my books that sold the most copies).
  - o When I released one book all the page numbers in the paperbacks table of contents showed as "4", something as silly as not updating the page numbers in the TOC when I made a minor change meant that this version was live for 6 weeks. I hadn't even noticed it in the proof copies I'd received but whenever anyone used the "look inside" feature on AMZ they could see that the page numbers

where wrong and that first impression meant no paperback sales.

Respect your reader

I was recently offered three people's books to read (and although there was no definitive expectation of a review, I like to help other authors).

I am unsure why but all three of the authors had English as a second language, this meant that there translations where more pigeon English than correct English.

I do not see myself as a "Grammar Nazi" but I felt the initial state of the books would be detrimental to the authors and their readers.

Rather than review the books in the current state, I offered to edit the books (for free). Two of the authors accepted my offer and were very happy with the edited manuscripts.

The third author had written a short quotes book that was basically one long list of quotes. The formatting was all over the place and although it wouldn't have taken me long to tidy it up, the author declined my offer because he believed (and stated) that it didn't matter because it would only be priced at $0.99 on Amazon, so people wouldn't care.

Your readers deserve better!

- Whatever price your book is to be priced at (even if it is Perma–Free), you must understand that a reader is committing more than just money to your book.
- When a reader chooses a book they are committing their valuable time to read it and time is a finite commodity. It is, therefore, your responsibility to provide the best book that you possibly can for your readers.

The KDP Platform Content Tab

The first time that you upload a manuscript to KDP it can be quite stressful. Once you have actually got your book live and you find an issue in your Kindle book (this happens more often than not), it can feel even more stressful trying to update your book contents.

To help mitigate your stress, I have laid out this section as per the "Kindle eBook Content" tab on the KDP platform.

Manuscript

There are only two parts to this section of the Tab:

- Digital Rights Management (DRM)

DRM is a copyright protection for digital media and is designed to prevent unauthorized distribution by restricting the way consumers can copy content that they have purchased.

The KDP system gives you the option to Enable DRM (by ticking the circle at the side of "Yes" or "No"). Once you have published your book, you cannot change its DRM settings on KDP. Enabling DRM in this system can provide you some peace of mind. I must warn you that once your book is out there in the real world it is relatively easy for nefarious individuals to pirate your information (I state this not to scaremonger but to make you aware of this possibility).

- Upload eBook Manuscript

When you click on the big yellow button (marked "Upload eBook Manuscript") the process is very similar to attaching a document to an email. You just choose the document and upload it for processing. It can take a couple of minutes to process but you can work in other sections of the input process, whilst this is happening.

Kindle eBook Previewer

Once the platform has finished processing the manuscript you uploaded, it provides you two ways to preview what it looks like.

- Online Previewer

Simply clicking on the "Launch Previewer" button allows you to see what the book will look like on a digital device.

This method is the best option for me as it allows me to view on a big screen and is easy to navigate through.

- Downloadable Preview Options

If you prefer to preview on your own Kindle or computer this option allows you to do that.

The instructions are pretty self-explanatory but even if you are going to review your book with the online previewer, I still use this option to download a mobi version of my book. Having a mobi version of your book allows you to check how any updates look on your Kindle and also provides you ARC copies for distribution.

Simply click on the hyperlink titled "mobi" from either of the drop-down menus ("preview on your computer" or "preview on your Kindle device") and save the "Kindle content" file somewhere on your computer. I tend to rename the file with the name of the book, the date of the download and that this is the kindle version of the book.

As you start to publish and update your books it is important to have a filing system to keep track of the various versions of your book.

Emailing an updated mobi file to your Kindle, every time you make a minor change is not advisable as it can get very confusing on your device. Remember that this will show in your Kindle library as a "doc" and not a "book".

Kindle eBook Cover
There are two options here:

- Use KDP's Cover creator

The KDP platform allows you to create a cover using your own images (or stock images). If you decide to use their creator then please follow the instructions, I will not be covering that here.

- Upload a cover you already have

Just as with the Manuscript uploader, when you click on the big yellow button (this time marked "Upload your cover file") the process is very similar to attaching a document to an email. You just choose the image and upload it for processing.

You must ensure that the Image meets the guidelines (e.g. 2,560 pixels high by 1,600 pixels wide. I'll discuss the specifications of book covers more in the chapter on book covers, as Amazon can change their guidelines check that your image meets their current guidelines.

Kindle eBook ISBN

In this section the platform provides you two places to input your book's information:

- ISBN

As eBooks don't require an International Standard Book Number (ISBN). As an Indie author, you can leave this optional field blank.

- Publisher

The system allows for traditional Publishers (as well as Self-Publishers) to upload manuscripts. As an Indie author, you can leave this optional field blank.

A Final Thought borrowed from Stephen King

Writing a lot of content may seem the obvious first step but lots of words don't make a story.

I love the story that Stephen King recounts about James Joyce (I apologize for paraphrasing):

- "A Friend came to visit Joyce one day and found the great man sprawled across his writing desk in a posture of utter despair.
- 'James, what's wrong?' the friend asked. 'Is it work?'
- Joyce indicated assent without even raising his head to look at his friend. Of course, it was the work; wasn't it always?
- 'How many words did you get today?' the friend pursued.
- Joyce (still in despair, still sprawled face down on his desk) replied 'Seven.'
- 'Seven? But James... that's good, at least for you.'
- 'Yes,' Joyce said, finally looking up. 'I suppose it is... but I don't know what order they go in!"

Although the content is important (and the lack of inspiration can be used for procrastination) I want you to think of this seven words tale whenever you become solely focused on just throwing words onto the page.

Exercises

You need to determine which processes and systems you are going to use to ensure the quality of your book's content. The writing process can be time-consuming so for the sake of efficiency, start with the end in mind.

I had personally started writing this book in MS Word and then tried to switch to Scrivener.

As I had already created almost 70% of the content when I chose to change, I ended up switching back to Word.

Exercise Eight   Determine the Format for Writing Your Book
You can choose Scrivener MS Word, Google docs etc. but I suggest that you decide from the offset which you will use.

Although we are in the early stages of your book, for efficiency it is best to start with the end in mind. You may change certain things as you work through the process but the exercises below are designed to help provide you an overview and starting point.

Rather than just decide how you will write your book, you need to take some action.

Some options for those actions are:

- Open a folder on your computer and start to populate it with MS Word docs & a tracking spreadsheet.
- Create a Google account and Open a google doc & a Google sheet in your Google drive.
- Purchase Scrivener & Open a new project in Scrivener for your book.

Whichever format you decide to use, don't make a decision without taking some action. Before you leave this exercise, carry out at least two tasks (relating to this format) to move your book forward.

Exercise Nine   Determine your Research Process
Whether you are writing Fiction or Non-Fiction you will need to have some methods for research.

Although your budget may be a big determining factor in which method you use, here are some Suggestions:

- Research all of your content through online searches.
- Research all of your content through books.
- Research all of your content by traveling and interacting with people.
- Research your content using a hybrid of all of the options above (If you are choosing this option, determine what percentage of each of the methods you will use to produce your content).

Whichever research process you decide to use, don't make a decision without taking some action. You will need to track your research so set up a tracking system for this research, before leaving this exercise.

Exercise Ten   Determine your Editing Process

You need to decide if you need all four types of editor for your book and consider where you will source any relevant editors.

Points to consider:

- What is your Editing budget?
- Who do you know that may edit at a discount?
- Do you have anyone who would provide a final proofread for you?
- How much notice will your editors /proof-readers require before your publishing deadline?

Before you leave this exercise, write down which of the four types of editing that you are going to employ. For each of the types of editing that you decide to use, write down two sources or options that you will use to achieve this edit.

Chapter 5 The Book Cover

"A book cover is a distillation. It is a haiku of the story." — **Chip Kidd**

Whenever you see an article, blog or book concerning book covers, they tend to mention the old cliché "Never judge a book by its cover". That statement may be useful when we are talking about not prejudging people but when it comes to books, people do judge them by their first impression of the cover.

You want your cover to draw attention to your book and pique the interest of potential readers, to make them want to know more about the book. Certain elements such as the colour of your book cover can repel a reader before they even get a chance to read the book title.

Packaging
There is a reason why multinational companies spend millions of dollars on package design for their products because they realize that the packaging helps sell their products.

Although most indie authors may not have a huge budget to spend on their book cover design, it is worth noting that your book cover is the packaging for your book.

You may believe that you have written an amazing book but if your cover doesn't encourage the reader to look inside, you have actually written a load of secrets (for no-one to read).

As you read through this chapter please keep one fact in the back of your mind. Your book cover is an advertisement for the contents of your book!

Look At Your Opposition

If you look at the top sellers in your niche or genre there is a good chance that they are doing things right.

Why wouldn't you mirror the successful elements of their book covers?

I'll cover images further in this chapter but:

- If you enter the search term "romance novels" into the Amazon search bar you will notice that a lot of the book covers have an image of a semi-clad male on the front.
- Typing in "Western Novels" into the Amazon search bar you will notice that a lot of the book covers have images of cowboys on the front cover.

The reason for these commonalities is that the images identify the genre before the readers even read the title. If you are going to write in these genres wouldn't it make sense to ensure that your book cover maintains a similar theme?

The Cost of Your Cover

As an indie author (as we discussed in the chapter on budgets) you have to weigh up the return on investment in relation to any publishing costs for your book.

It's your choice:

- Are you going to pay a professional designer for your book cover?
- Are you going to find a cheap designer on Fiverr?

- Are you going to choose an option somewhere in between?

Just because you pay $500 for a book cover you may not get a better result than paying $10 for the same cover. Some authors pay the higher price because they believe that the designer will produce a better cover. Some authors choose the higher price because they believe that they will get more guidance from the designer.

When you are first starting out as an indie author, you may not realize that you are the person that makes the final decision on the cover. However much you decide to pay for the design, you will still have to choose the final edit.

After serving twenty-two years in the military, my haircut has tended to remain the same. I either have a buzz cut number two or a buzz cut number three and this makes my instructions to the barber (or hairdresser) straightforward. Even with my simple haircut, I still need to tell them what I want

Would you ever go into a new hairdresser and say "just do whatever you feel like to my hair?" I'm assuming that you give them some instructions? Likewise, you need to have some concept of your book cover before you contact your designer.

If you just say to a designer "do whatever you want for my book cover", there is a very high probability that you will be disappointed with the results.

N.B. If you are planning on using certain websites such as Bookbub.com they require a professional looking cover before they will let you pay them to promote your book.

Briefing Designers / Virtual Assistants

Having used multiple Virtual assistants (VA's) on Upwork and Fiverr for design work in the past, I understand the importance of providing them a detailed brief.

We should never assume that a designer can read our mind and even when the designer speaks the same language as us, we must ensure that we are precise with our instructions.

Even if you have used a designer previously, don't assume that they will know what you want in any new designs.

As this book is aimed at publishing your Kindle book on KDP, you only need a front cover to upload. If your intention is to publish a paperback version of your book (and it makes sense to launch both formats at the same time), ensure that you include the requirements for the pdf of your full print cover in your brief.

I personally have a graphics VA who is fast and efficient. In order to give myself a few extra design options, I tend to task the same front cover design to three designers on Upwork / Fiverr.

Once I receive the three completed designs I progress in one of two ways.

1. I choose to keep the best design and task my VA to adapt it for my paperback and other book format covers
2. I choose the best elements from the three designs and task my VA to adapt them for the finished book cover (including my paperback and other book format covers).

If you are going to pay a VA on Fiverr or Upwork for a design ensure that you give them a detailed brief:

- They must ensure that any images that they use are royalty free. (See the resources section at the back of the book for some suggested royalty free sites).

- Be precise about the format that the book cover is to be supplied in. Do you want jpeg, Png, Pdf, etc?
- Be precise about the other specifications of the cover, ratio of the image 1:6 width to height etc.
- If you want a specific Font let them know (there can also be a royalty issue here).
- Some of the designers will require you to choose a stock image (if they direct you to a stock photo site be prepared to choose an image).
- If you are going to use colours as part of your brand (as Robert Kiyosaki did with his Black & Purple for Rich Dad / Poor Dad), ensure that you tell them what colours you want. If like me you can't tell the difference between two shades of brown (such as rich biscuit and dark cumin) ensure that you give them the specific colour code.
- There are a multitude of colour charts online (typing a Search term such as "Brown colour code" in google and you will get several options), I tend to take a screenshot of the specific colour chart and send it to the designer with the code.

Set realistic expectations, even if you give a thorough brief, the chances are that you will still need some minor revisions to the first cover design they provide.

Some designers allow unlimited revisions and some may have a limit of only three revisions in their initial price. Ensure you know the specific details of any contractual agreement with a VA (whatever your budget is).

Although my evidence is only from my personal experience (and other authors I have worked with), It is rare that anyone gets a perfect design on the first attempt.

I have provided examples of templates and sample briefs at Appendix E of this book. This will provide you further direction in the information you will need for your designer brief.

Colour Choices

When you are choosing a colour for your book it is a balancing act between making your book distinct enough to attract attention and not being too dazzling that you repulse viewers.

Contrast

Whether you choose light coloured text on a dark background or dark coloured text on a light background, you need to take into account how these will contrast in grey scale (when your book cover is viewed in black and white).

Some colour combinations may be easy to discern in a colour thumbnail on Amazon's storefront but can be harder to discern when viewed as a black and white thumbnail on a kindle paper.

A high percentage of Kindle owners now purchase on their devices, and as they will be viewing your book cover in greyscale, you need to consider how your choice of colours will contrast when viewed in black and white.

The Science of Colour

The science of colour is an interesting but detailed subject, so for the purpose of this section, I shall just provide an overview to help you understand some basic concepts.

Individually we tend to have a preference for certain colours in our lives. Although we may think that this is just our way of expressing ourselves, there are some scientific studies that explain that the neurons in our brains may actually be chemically designed to react to certain colours.

I don't purport to have any qualifications in neuroscience but from several years of marketing in various forms, I recognize that some colours instinctively attract us and others instinctively repulse us.

Bees
It is believed that one of the reasons that bees are yellow and black is that their contrasting stripes serve as a warning to birds not to eat them. Other colours such as red are also known to be physiologically / neurally stimulating in ways that can make us avoid them.

I am old enough to remember posting fliers in people's letterboxes for a home-based business. At one sales show, I printed the same information on yellow, red and green paper.

It might seem an anecdotal study but I still remember the different physical reactions of individuals being handed different coloured fliers. With the yellow fliers, some recipients actually changed their facial expressions.

Stop Signs
From 1924 to 1954 Road traffic Stop Signs (in the USA) were yellow and black but they changed to the current red colouring to provide uniformity with red traffic lights (Red meaning stop).

Clearly, we are not only hard-wired to react to certain colours but the world around us also affects how we react to them.

It is worth bearing this in mind when you choose colours for your book covers.

Images
There is a reason that the saying "A picture paints a thousand words" (or derivatives thereof) has remained relevant for over one hundred years. Just one look at a picture can tell us so much about the subject that it relates to.

As well as being eye-catching your book cover also needs to be relevant:

- If a book cover has a picture of a figure in a space suit, stood in front of a spaceship, holding some kind of gun on the front, we would assume that this book is a Science fiction book. We would also assume that there is some kind of conflict on a planet where humans need to wear space suits.
- If a book cover has the image of a jockey on a horse in his silks, we automatically assume that the book content is in some way centered on horse racing.
- Images of lots of bank notes tell us that there are some financial components to the book's content.
- If you are writing a book about guns, I would surmise that you may have a selection of guns on the cover (not a selection of shoes).

All those images frame a story before we have even added one word to the book cover.

Even the expression on someone's face on a book cover can portray a variety of emotions, from fear and happiness to even menace.

Rather than just filling this book with specifics of which images relate best to specific genres, I want you to focus on your personal book cover.

In this short introduction to book cover images, I encourage you to examine if the images you choose help to support the content of your book.

Image Restrictions
As well as making your images relevant there are a few issues that you should consider before making the final choice of an image for your book cover.

- Ensure that there are no issues with royalty rights for your images. Just because an image is classed as royalty free for some usage doesn't mean that is also royalty free for publication. Ideally, source the image yourself and supply it to the designer.
- Be aware that if your images are classed as too racy or contentious this may impact your ability to promote your book. Certain platforms such as Facebook will not allow adult-rated content in their Ads.
- Using someone's image without their permission is a really bad idea. This is not just images of people but images of logos or anything that someone else owns the Intellectual property for.
- Even photographs of some modern buildings can actually be restricted as the architect may have copyright on them.

The Book Title

The next chapter in this book is devoted to the book's title so I will only mention it briefly here.

When we think about the book cover we need to understand that the book title is a key element of that cover and consider that:

- The Title and any images on the cover need to support each other.
- An amazing colourful image may look great but can make the title hard to read when viewed in certain formats.
- We must ensure the text is legible, making it look rustic or historical may seem artistic but if you can't read it, it's not text.

Text and Name Placement

Whether you are writing under your own name or a Pen name (pseudonym), the placement of the author's name on the cover can be important.

The more well-known you become the more your name can be a brand and you may choose to place your name at the top of the book rather than in small print at the bottom.

If you look at a book by the likes of Tony Robbins or Stephen King you will see that their name is as prominent (if not more prominent) than the book title. This is because they have name recognition and their name sells books as much as the book title.

Authors sometimes have an issue with self-promotion but as you produce more books, you want people to identify your titles at a glance.

Even if you don't perceive that you have name recognition for your first book, ensure that your name is large enough to read. Future books can increase sales of your current books so you want to ensure that they can read your name now as well as in the future.

Pen (Pseudonyms) Names
There are several reasons why writers choose to publish under a pen name:

- If they switch publishers and their previous publisher owns the rights to an upcoming work under their name.
- If a previous literary work failed miserably (and they want to distance themselves from it).
- They want a name that resonates more with a specific genre, fantasy, erotica etc.
- They want some level of anonymity if a genre is seen as contentious.

The same guidelines for name placement apply to Pen Names as with an author's given names.

Remember that writing under a Pen name does not mean that you don't want brand recognition, it is just a different brand that you are trying to build.

Novelty

When we consider a book cover such as purple cow by (master marketer) Seth Godin, it is a novel book cover that stands out from the crowd. As the premise of the book centers around standing out like a purple cow in the middle of a herd of black and white cows, that is what you would expect.

We should note that Seth didn't just throw this book title out there. One of Seth's genius marketing tactics was to send out 4000 pre-publication paperback copies of the book in milk cartons. The milk cartons had the same purple cow pattern as the book covers and this helped to create some recognition and buzz for the book (and its cover).

General Notes on Layout

If you choose to write a book on minimalism, you may want a nice clean minimal cover and it may have no images.

The JPEG / TIFF that you upload to the KDP platform has to meet the same technical specification for Fiction and Non-Fiction.

A design for a fantasy fiction cover will usually require more work than a basic Non-Fiction cover.

International Standard Book Number (ISBN)

New Authors sometimes worry about the requirement for ISBN's for their Kindle books.

We are used to seeing an ISBN on the back of print books but there is no requirement for the ISBN to be listed on a digital

Although each book has a unique identifier to allow publishers around the world to identify their work (and to allow tracking of the books worldwide), Amazon uses its own tracking system (ASIN's) to track the kindle versions of books. An ASIN (Amazon Standard

Identification Number) is a way for Amazon to track all of the products in their inventory. Here we go again classing your book as a product!

Amazon actually allocates an ASIN to your book when you list it.

This ASIN only applies to the Kindle version of your book so should you want to publish a physical copy of your book it requires an ISBN.

Back Cover Text
Although this book is designed for writers publishing on Kindle, as lots of indie publishers will also publish a print version, I want to briefly cover this element of the book cover.

The back text is an extra way to market your book and even when selling print copies on Amazon, their platform allows you to view the text on the back copy.

A few points to consider for this Back Cover Text:

- Some authors tend to provide an excerpt of the book content in the text but that is not always the best way to engage readers.
- Less is more. The back cover of a book requires the art of copywriting so be engaging but succinct.
- If you intend to stretch an intricate front image around to the back cover of a book ensure that the text is still legible. One option here is to place a text box over the rear image with a plain background.
- If you are fortunate enough to have a review or a quote for your book from a celebrity (or influencer), this should be included on the back cover as well as inside the book.

Changing Your Cover
It's recognized that if you have a "bad" book cover and you improve the cover, it is one of the factors that can improve sales of that book.

I have to admit that I have never seen myself as very creative and so I never thought much about the whole area of designs and colours.

Maybe my lack of colour nuance was partly due to twenty plus years of wearing green and camouflage (in the military).

When I published my first book I just looked at the other books in my niche and tried to pick out the best elements and recognizable colours. And it took me some time of submissions and revisions with a designer to get to my finished product.

As an Indie writer, we may be more involved in the elements of our book than someone who publishes through a traditional publishing company. We don't have our own design department so we may be out of our comfort zone.

Once you've gone through the ordeal of choosing your cover you can become attached to it but I want you to recognize your book cover for what it is. Your book cover is an advertising tool.

Changing the Advertisement
As I said at the start of this chapter "your book cover is an advertisement for the contents of your book".

One of the Cardinal rules of advertising (sometimes referred to as the seven times factor), is that potential customers need to see an Ad seven times before they notice it.

This factor doesn't state that they will buy after seven exposures but will notice the Ad. If it's a bad advertisement they may then decide not to buy the product.

Once you have realized that the book cover is just an advertisement, it can make it easier to change that cover if it is not working.

Writers tend to get emotional about all of the elements of their books (including the cover), which is why any editing decisions can be painful.

I encourage you to get emotional about your book cover but only if you change it and it increases book sales. If your book isn't selling and by changing your cover, you sell lots more books, then feel free to jump up and down.

Resistance

I have to confess that while I was writing this book I was fortunate to have Jonathan Green (of Serve no Master) take a look at the cover of one of my other books. I knew that he was going to say it was too bright but even after his feedback I didn't really want to change it.

Although I wasn't invested emotionally in that books cover I had invested some time in its choice.

During my initial colour choice, I had split tested several colour options for that book cover (over several weeks) in order to choose the most appealing colour prior to publishing.

I wanted to share this with you because even though I knew Jonathan was right, it was only by taking the emotion out of the decision that I forced myself to change the colour of the book cover.

Amazon Isn't Perfect

If you update a new cover for your book you need to monitor your listing until it is correct and if there is an issue, contact Amazon immediately.

Although this book is mainly focused on Kindle publishing, I assume that you will be publishing a paperback at some time and have all the formats of your book linked on the same listing.

There can sometimes be a delay in the updating of all of your listings, this means that your Kindle book cover and your paperback etc. may not be the same (until everything is sorted).

If you see a problem don't wait, contact them immediately. Any delays are potentially costing you sales.

I updated one of my book covers from fluorescent green to dark green and at one stage the front of the paperback was showing as dark green and the back was fluorescent. Yes, this was only on the Amazon listing (and not the printed book) but who would buy a book if they thought that was the final product?

N.B. I have provided an Annex at the back of this book with some examples of briefs for designers. Some designers may allow you the ability to cut and paste the whole brief and others may have a template for you to add this information piecemeal. I advise you to check out this information before contacting your designer.

Exercises

When the time comes to design your own book cover, it can take longer than you expect.

The exercise here is designed to allow you to become comfortable with the design process prior to tasking someone to design your own cover.

Exercise Eleven   Writing a Brief for an Existing Book Cover

Search on Amazon in your current book genre and choose a specific book cover from those listed.

Using the template and sample briefs in Appendix E, complete a brief for the designer of this book cover.

As you already have the completed book cover as a reference this should be easier than designing your own cover from your own imagination.

- Identify where the title ends and the sub-title starts.
- Take a screenshot of similar book covers in this genre and look for commonalities.

- For any colours search the web for a colour chart and pick the closest code to that colour (quoting the code and screenshotting the chart).

Exercise Twelve   Writing a Brief for Your Book Cover
Now that you are more experienced with the process of cover design, you can start to work on your own book cover.

Using the template and sample briefs in Appendix E, complete a brief for the designer for your own book cover.

- If you have already completed your initial design for your book cover you may want to work through this exercise to see if you have missed anything.
- Ensure your book cover is relevant to your genre.

NB.   Don't let your search for the perfect cover stop you publishing your book.

Chapter 6 The Book Title

"It's not how big your pencil is; it's how you write your name." —
David Mustaine

The Purpose of a Book Title

The Book title and the way that it is displayed on the cover form part of your book's first impression with your readers. It's up to you whether that first impression is memorable in either a positive or negative way.

The purpose of a book title is to peak the reader's interest and to help them make a decision that the book is going to meet their requirements. The title of your book is, therefore, one of the key sales elements of your book.

Famous and Fortunate

If you are extremely famous (such as Stephen King or J.K. Rowling) you could possibly publish your grocery shopping list, title it "my grocery list" and still sell lots of copies.

One of the points to note here is that the names of these famous authors are actually huge brands. Those brands are part of a large marketing machine that has taken time to build.

When you take into account that Rowling's first Harry Potter manuscript was turned down by 12 publishing houses you can see that we all have to start somewhere.

For those authors that are not household names, we need to work a little harder on the composition of our book titles.

Factors When Choosing Your Book Title

- How Will Readers Find Your Book?
- How Will Readers View Your Book Title?
- Does Your Book Title Peak a Reader's Interest?
- What Do the Words Tell the Reader about the Book's Contents?
- Does it Match Their Favourite Author or Genre?
- Are There Any Offensive or Distasteful Words in Your Book Title?

How Will Readers Find Your Book?

Although it would be fantastic if the title of your book magically popped into a reader's head and they were then magically taken to the Amazon checkout (with your book selected), this doesn't happen.

You may have used marketing tools (such as Facebook ads, website competitions etc.) to raise awareness of your book but an Amazon customer will usually find you because they were already on Amazon's platform. While on Amazon, the algorithm may have displayed a thumbnail of your book cover on the page.

The Amazon system displays your book due to either organic or paid methods.

Organic Methods

For this category, organic refers to a naturally occurring display due to your search term triggering a match with certain parts of the Amazon algorithm.

This algorithm is basically a sorting program that is weighted in certain ways to provide the best match for a customer's search. There are only so many books that they can display on one page so the books have to be sorted and ranked.

Although no one knows the exact weighting of the Amazon algorithm there are certain things that are widely accepted as influencing search results:

- Keyword match — It might seem obvious but the closer your words match the words typed into a search box, the higher your chances of your book being displayed.
- Amazon Seller ranking — If your book isn't selling well for a prolonged period it can fall so far down the ranking that even if your keywords match, it won't show in searches.
- Also Viewed — There is also a section on the Amazon page for "customers who viewed this item also viewed". If you have several books in the same niche or genre, one of your books may actually be promoting another in the same niche or genre.

Paid Methods

Authors can promote their books on the Amazon system so that their book is displayed when a customer searches by keywords.

Authors can also promote their books via interests so that Kindle owners (who allow ads on their Kindle e-reader) that match certain criteria, have your book displayed in full screen when they turn on their Kindle.

We will cover Amazon Ads in a later chapter but the main thing I want you to consider here is that there are several ways that Amazon customers can find your books. When we combine how they find your book, with how they will view your book title, this makes for important considerations.

How Will Readers View Your Book Title?

Other than an Amazon display ad (that shows the full book cover on their Kindle) most book covers will be displayed as a thumbnail image.

If a customer is searching on their computer or a large screen your book cover may show up as an image that is only two or three inches high. Because lots of readers are now searching on their mobile devices, the image that they see may be even smaller.

When we factor in the customers who search directly from their Kindle, they could be viewing a small book cover in black and white.

It is therefore important that the title is legible in a small font.

Font
When we are choosing a font for the title (or any other text) on our book cover, the ultimate choice is ours.

Although this can relate to price (Some discount designers may not have access to more expensive fonts), the use of some fonts can look messy if they are not done professionally.

Individuals don't always realize that (just as with images) some fonts need to be purchased and have royalty rights attached to them. It's your responsibility to check this out before you publish your book as your discount designer may not.

Some of the suggested fonts (that you probably won't find on your MS Word drop-down menu):

- For business books, "Baskerville" or "League Gothic" can produce some good results.
- Thrillers or Mysteries can look good in "Franchise"
- Historical Fiction can look good in "Trajan" or "Baskerville".
 You can find a wide selection of paid and free fonts on sites such as 1001fonts.com or Fontsquirell.com

There are no hard and fast rules as to which Fonts you should use. Once again, look at the other books in your genre and see what the successful other books are using.

I tend to get the designer to give me three font options of the same book title and then beta test them. Remember that you need to choose your audience so don't ask in a Facebook group on Stock Trading for participants to choose the font for a book on erotica.

A few questions to consider:

- Can you read the words on your book cover in a thumbnail (if it is displayed in the search results on Amazon etc.)?
- A white text might look artistic but is your background dark enough to contrast and make it legible? White writing against a grey background can make it harder to read.
- How would your text look in greyscale (a lot of people buy on a Kindle and a black and white thumbnail may look different to a coloured one)?

Title / Subtitle
Single Word (or very short) Book titles are popular in some niches. This allows your title to be read when viewed in a smaller image but doesn't always tell the reader what the book is about.

Shorter Titles also make it harder to include Keywords (which can be important for feeding the Amazon search algorithm) so Subtitles are becoming more important.

The Book's subtitle can provide clarification on the subject matter as well as providing the opportunity to include some useful keywords.

Consider A book with the main Title "Stock Options Trading", which of the following subtitles would you choose:

- The Martians have landed.   —   Although this subtitle may be quirky it is probably not relevant to this book and there are no useful keywords to feed the search algorithm.
- What's it all about?   —   This might have made a good Main title, to peak the reader's interest but it seems to be asking

the reader the question rather than telling them that the book provides the answer.

- A Beginners Guide to profitable day trading. — This Subtitle informs the reader that the book is for beginners and is aimed at day trading, these are also useful search keywords and the word profitable is also a useful search keyword.

When you are choosing your own sub-titles you may have options with less obvious differences than the three examples above. The reason I have provided examples with such stark contrasts, is to allow you to focus on the specific elements when choosing your own subtitles.

Does Your Book Title Peak a Reader's Interest?

Tim Ferriss has published several books such as "The 4 Hour Work Week" and "The 4 Hour Body" which automatically gel with people's view of being Time Poor.

Even though readers are becoming savvier to marketing tricks, titles like "The Monk Who Sold His Ferrari" or "Purple Cow" can make us take a second look.

The trick is to keep a reader's attention once your title has caught it.

What Do the Words Tell the Reader about the Book's Contents?

Non - Fiction – Does the title tell the reader it has the answer that will solve their issue? If they are looking to earn money online, the title could be something like "How to earn $10,000 in 30 days online". If they are searching for Churchill's life story, the title could be something like "The Untold Autobiography of Winston Churchill".

For Fiction – Does the title match the genre? If they are searching for sword and sorcery, fantasy a title like "The Chronicle of the magician's sword" lets them identify that this matches their genre. The title doesn't have to contain the exact words relating to sword and sorcery but I offer this example for simplification (So you get the idea).

Does it Match Their Favourite Author or Genre?

If you are extremely famous (such as Stephen King or J.K. Rowling) you could possibly publish your grocery shopping list, title it "my grocery list" and still sell lots of copies.

One of the points to note here is that the names of famous authors are actually huge brands. Those brands are part of a large marketing machine that has taken time to build.

When you take into account that Rowling's first Harry Potter manuscript was turned down by 12 publishing houses you can see that we all have to start somewhere.

Are There Any Offensive or Distasteful Words in Your Book Title?

Some authors such as Jen Sincero have built a brand around being authentic. One of the ways that they display their authenticity is by using words and terms that are not traditionally used in polite society.

Although you may feel that this type of authenticity matches your brand, be cautious in the words you use in your book title.

Some Impolite words may not stop your book being listed on Amazon but can have negative issues for marketing:

- The current or future terms on social media platforms may reject Ad campaigns containing your book title. As a lot of these platforms use algorithms to check campaigns, dubious words can cause rejection automatically.

- Amazon book reviews can be rejected for your book. Automation may mean that the words in your book title are flagged by the algorithm and stop that review being accepted.

Exercises

Depending on what stage you are in your publishing journey, you may have already achieved the results in some of these exercises. Read the exercises and determine which are relevant to you.

Exercise Thirteen   Choosing a Working Title

Choose a working title for your book. Although you probably have some vague title when you refer to your work, just calling it "The Book" is not very productive.

Choosing something a little closer to the subject matter of the book can help keep you on track with the premise of the book (subject matter). Calling your book "How to make $30,000 from property flipping" or "The tale of the dragon who became a princess" will keep the main subject of the book, front of mind.

Exercise Fourteen   Beta Testing Your Book Titles

Narrow your book title down to three options and then ask for feedback on which title is more likely to pique reader's interest.

- You can test the titles by asking for feedback or setting up a survey on Twitter, Facebook or some other social media platform.
- Ensure that you write the titles in the same font type and size, to avoid variations unduly influencing respondents.
- Try to test your titles in audiences that may read this genre of book.
- Choose the title with the highest feedback. If the top two are close then carry out another test with just those top two titles.

Chapter 7 The Book Details and Listing Description

"The aim of marketing is to know and understand the customer so well the product or service fits him and sells itself." — **Peter Drucker**

Landing Pages

The key thing to bear in mind is that your Amazon book listing is a "Landing Page".

A Landing Page is traditionally the first online page (on a website or as a standalone) that someone lands on when they click a link or type in your web address. It is designed to convert the reader from a prospective buyer to an actual buyer of a product.

Whether a prospective buyer is sent to this page from an online Ad, a webinar or any other means of promotion, this is the page that you want them to Land on (hence the term Landing Page) and this page's primary purpose is to get them to buy.

The key component of any product is the benefits that it provides to the customer and Landing Pages highlight these benefits.

Amazon Landing Pages have some of the best conversion rates (of prospects to buyers) in the world, as customers are coming to the site to buy. When you add buyers to a site whose primary purpose is to sell products, it is like adding oil to a fire.

Although buyers are looking to purchase it doesn't mean that they want to buy your product (book).

Amazon Listings

Once your amazing book cover and catchy book title have caught a reader's attention, you need to capitalize on that and make sure that your reader engages with your description.

Your book description needs to stand out from the rest!

When I first started selling physical products on Amazon.com, one of the easiest ways to increase sales was to have a better description and nicer pictures than your competitors (even with almost identical products). I know I keep emphasizing that your book is a product but when authors refuse to accept this, they are restricting their sales.

An engaging listing works for your book just like any other product listed on Amazon, your reader needs to know "what's in it for them".

When you are listing your first book in your KDP dashboard it can seem a little daunting but if you work through it methodically (and take note of the information in this chapter), you will find that it's not that difficult.

KDP Tab Layout

The main elements to focus on in this chapter are the text in your book description and the keywords. To simplify things I have laid out the contents of this section in the same order that it currently appears in the "input eBook details" section of KDP.

Language

Most Authors listing on Amazon.com will leave this as the default "English" setting but I always double check that the correct language is set before I move on.

Book Titles

As this book includes a whole chapter on your book title, the only reason we mention the subject here is to ensure that you input the correct information when listing your book for publication.

You may have been writing your book under a working title so ensure that when you complete the Book title and subtitle fields, you are using the same details that you have displayed on your book cover.

If you decide to publish a physical print version of your book through Create space etc., ensure that you list the book under exactly the same title and subtitle in both your KDP Listing and Createspace Listing. I once accidentally missed an apostrophe off a word when creating one of my listings, this meant the sub-titles in the two listings were slightly different.

Even though I corrected my error the next day, I had to actually contact Createspace and this delayed the print and Kindle versions of the book being linked on Amazon. When both listings are linked the reviews for them both are displayed together in the books total reviews.

Series

Although this may be your first book as an indie writer, you may have already determined that it is part of a series. You can go back and update this section later so if it's your first book, just leave it blank.

It is worth noting that Non-Fiction books can also be part of a series. When you complete this section of your book description the information will be displayed along with your book title.

For My Book "Gratitude for Happiness" I grouped it with my book "527 quotes for Entrepreneurs" into the Inspiration Series. The title now displayed on the Amazon book listing is "Gratitude for Happiness: How to exercise your gratitude muscles (Inspiration Series Book 1)".

As the words in brackets indicate that this is "Book 1" in a series, it is telling a reader that there are more books available in that series and each book is helping to promote other books in the same series.

Author

This is the name that will appear in your book's listing and will help you claim your book for your bibliography. If you are writing under a Pen name or a variation of your name for different genres, ensure that you complete the correct details in here.

Some successful authors such as Joanna Penn, have separate author names for their Fiction and Non-Fiction (i.e. she writes her Fiction under J.F. Penn). By providing a delineation between the two genres it can help you optimize the Amazon algorithm. Remember the algorithm determines where, when and with which other books it displays your books.

Contributors

As an indie author, I usually list my editor, cover designer etc. in the dedications page of my book. Unless you are co-writing a book with another author, you are probably going to leave these contributor fields blank.

Description

This is one of the most important sections of your books as the description is a critical part of the book sales funnel.

If a reader goes to a brick and mortar bookstore to purchase a book, they can physically pick up the book and connect with it with all of their senses. For online purchases your reader is deprived of that physical connection, so you need to paint a picture of your book with the words in your description.

Amazon provides the look inside feature and the potential to download a sample of your book. Unless your description engages a reader, they may never progress to those features with your book.

Remember that the focus of a Landing page is on the benefits of the product to the customer and your book description should promote your book's benefits:

- For Non-fiction such as "How To" books, we are highlighting the way the book will solve the reader's problem. If a book is about making a million dollars in a week to create financial freedom, we may highlight the short timeframe and the amount of money.
- For Fiction, most readers are looking for some escapism so we want them to engage with the location, the characters or other aspects of the book that will make them want to immerse themselves in its pages.

The Hook

One of my favourite exercises is something that I adopted from Bryan Cohen. If you haven't heard of Bryan, he's a best-selling author of some great books such as "How to Write a Sizzling synopsis" (A book I highly recommend).

He suggests that you write twenty different versions of the hook for your book and then narrow those twenty down to the best one.

If you don't know what the hook is:

- The Hook is the text at the top of your Amazon book description.
- In well-formatted book descriptions, this is usually a larger font to draw attention to it.

- This tends to be about twenty to thirty words and is designed to grab the attention of the reader.
- When you click on an Amazon book listing, this is the only part of the book description that you can see (until you click on the "Read more" option).

Bryan suggests that a large percentage of readers will make the decision to buy your book, just by reading this portion of your book description.

Of course, you need a great book cover and book title to get them to this stage, but after reading the earlier chapters of this book I'm sure you've nailed them.

If you look at Bryan's Sizzling Synopsis book is hook reads:

 "Struggling to find new readers? Learn how a compelling synopsis can make your book fly off the digital shelves."

He managed to nail his hook in nineteen words by:

- Starting with a question to address the reader's issue. He reminds the book target market of authors that they have an issue of finding readers.
- He then supplies a solution to that problem (or pain point) by offering to show them how they can sell more books.

I'd surmise that if you are looking for a book on that subject, you wouldn't need to read much more to know that book meets your needs.

Content Text for your book Description
The text that you use for your book description is a method of marketing and should be written taking into consideration copywriting techniques.

Your text should be easy to read, attention-grabbing and relevant

- Make your initial heading something to catch the reader's attention:
    - An example for a Non-fiction book could be a call to action to read this book, such as "If you're ready to sell more books on Amazon, you must read this one now".
    - An example for a Fiction book could be a way of highlighting the content e.g. "For Fans of the Hunger Games" or "Number One on the Times bestsellers list".
- Make the subheading another enticement
    - For a Non-Fiction Book perhaps a question to the reader (about a problem) and ensure that the sentence points them to the subject of your book, to solve that problem.
    - For a Fiction Book start to introduce them to the wonders of your characters and settings.
- Use lists, bullet points and lots of white space to make the information easy to read (especially on mobile devices).
- Finish your text with another call to action:
    - For a Non-Fiction personal finance book, your final sentence could be something like "Buy this book now and start to make money in your sleep".
    - For a Fantasy fiction book perhaps something like "Buy this book and Come with me now to meet the amazing ice warriors as they battle the fire dragon in the wonderful land of Og".

Formatting the text

You might have noticed that a lot of the traditionally published books use very little formatting of their books description text.

As an indie author, one of the best ways to format your book description (to make it stand out) is using HTML code.

HTML is one of the computer codes that formats the way text is viewed online.

Unless you use HTML for your Amazon listing, the words will appear as basic unformatted text (this can make it seem bland and unappealing). Here's a short example of some of the code you will see in your listing (if you use HTML).

HTML Tag	Description
<b>	Formats the enclosed text as bold.
<font>	Determines the appearance of the enclosed text.
<u>	Formats the enclosed text as underlined.
<h1>	Formats the enclosed text as a section heading <h1> is the largest.
<h2>	Formats the enclosed text as a section heading <h2> is the next largest after <h1>.
<h3>	Formats the enclosed text as a section heading <h3> is the next largest after <h2>.

If like me you have no computer coding experience, it can seem a little daunting that you'll have to learn to code.

Fear not, as luckily there are (free) online tools that automatically create the code for you.

If you can use a basic word processor to format text, you can work with one of these code generators.

I highly recommend Dave Chesson's Code Generator over at the Kindlepreneur.com.

Once the code has been created you can cut and paste it straight into the description box of your book on the Kindle Direct Publishing (KDP) website.

If you are competent with HTML and decide to input the code yourself, only use the HTML codes that KDP allows.

Once your book listing is live on Amazon.com it will also be available on Amazon's other international sites and not all of the Amazon sites have the same CSS. CSS stands for Cascading Style Sheet and is one of the key technologies that determine the fonts, colours, and styles of text on a website.

All this talk of HTML and CSS is getting a bit technical so let me just simplify things a little. The main thing you need to know is that if your HTML code formats some text as a heading on Amazon.com, the text might be black but if Amazon.co.uk has a different CSS (and you use the same HTML code) it might display the heading in orange text.

Because of these potential differences in international sites, don't get too fancy with your HTML.

Inputting the Description text
When you want to change the text in your book (description) listing

Login to your KDP self-publishing account:

- Click on the "Bookshelf".
- Choose which of your books that you want to change the description for and click "Edit Details".
- Scroll down to the section titled "Description".
- Paste the code that was generated by the description generator (see the link above).
- Click "Save and Continue".
- Scroll down to the option "Save and Publish" and click on the button.

It can take 24 – 72hrs for this to update but once it's done. It's done.

Technical Specifications
The Maximum amount of Characters that you are allowed in the description box is 4,000 (that includes all HTML characters), that should give you plenty of characters for your description.

Once you have created your HTML code, if you highlight just the code, most word processors such as MS Word will display how many characters are in the code. If you have exceeded 4000 Characters, you need to change the text and generate a new code until it fits within the 4000 character parameters.

Categories

It is important that you ensure that you list your book in the correct category for various reasons:

- You can only list your book in a specific number of genres.
- Searchability. If someone types in "Romance novels and your romance novel is listed under "Westerns" it won't show up in the search.
- If your book is listed in the wrong category it may not just annoy readers in that category but if your book is being displayed and constantly being ignored, the Amazon algorithm will penalize your book and increase its Book Seller Ranking (BSR).
- If your book is listed in a less competitive category it may have a better chance of achieving best-seller status in that category. This benefit can be offset by the potential of a higher BSR as stated above.

As we discussed earlier in this book, your niche choice is important because you need to know who you are targeting your book to. When you decide how to categorize your book, you may feel disappointed with the options that the KDP platform presents you.

You may have seen other books listed in sub-genres that you can't find in the drop-down menus from the KDP dashboard.

Ideally, your book will fit into one of the available categories but if you want to access one of these hidden choices for your second category, here's how you do this:

- Select "Non-Classifiable" from the list of options available.

- Email KDP with the full category string that you wish your book to be listed under.
- E.g. Kindle Store>Kindle eBooks > Science Fiction & Fantasy > Science Fiction > Alien Invasion.

Remember that once your book is live you can get your book listed in extra categories (refer to chapter two in this book).

Book listing keywords

The KDP system provides you seven spaces for keywords when listing your book. The reason for this option is to help the right readers find your book. Although you might think it is gaining you extra exposure by using a common search term (even though it has no correlation to your book), if it is not putting your book in front of people likely to purchase it, the Amazon algorithm will not be happy.

The Keywords opportunity does allow you to bolster the ability for readers to find your book by allowing you to include search terms that are not included in the title of your book. E.g. if your book title is "Making $30,000 in Seven Days", it probably won't show if someone types in the keywords "how can I make lots of money?"

As you only have seven keyword spaces available, here are a few tips to optimize those spaces:

- You are not limited to one word in each of the Keyword spaces provided.
- You can post up to fifty characters in each space, so get creative and include sentences.
- If you do type a space between two words the system classes that as a character.
- Think of search terms that readers will type in when looking for your type of book.

- Don't waste your seven options by just duplicating words in the title of your book (they are already available in the title for searches).

I personally find that using software like KDP rocket can save you hours in choosing your keywords.

Age and Grade range

Choosing from the drop-down menus in this section is optional. For most authors, you will probably skip this section but if you are writing books for children or specific age groups it is important to input the information here.

Remember that the whole goal of KDP is to provide the best experience for their readers and sections like this allow Amazon to avoid exposing their audiences to inappropriate material.

Pre-Order

In the chapter on book launches, I cover Pre-orders in more depth but the main thing to note here is that you can leave the listing on the default setting of "I am ready to release my book now" and select the pre-order option at a later date.

Your book is not going to suddenly publish just because you have pressed save at this stage of inputting your book's information.

NB   The primary point to bear in mind is that the Amazon page for your book is actually a product landing page (designed to convert a person who lands on that page to make a purchase). The Amazon Landing page conversion rate is one of the best in the world.

Exercises

When you have your book draft formatted and ready to upload to KDP, you will have lots of activities to complete and may not have the mental bandwidth to take on all of the new skills. If you are just starting out on your publishing journey, now is the ideal time to do some preparation work.

Exercise Fifteen   Practicing With HTML

Choose six books in your genre, ideally, three written by well-known authors and three by not so famous authors.

I am assuming that if you are writing in a genre it is one that you traditionally read so you will know the big name authors in your genre. If not pick the top six books based on the number of reviews that they have.

- Pick at least one of these listings that hasn't been formatted with bold headings, bullet points, etc. and copy and paste the text into an HTML generator.
- Format the text a few times and copy and paste the code that the generator provides into a separate document.

This practice will make you comfortable using the tool and make it less daunting when you come to format your own text.

Exercise Sixteen   Confirming Your Keywords

It is important to remember that you are looking for additional keywords to those in your book title.

Although you are only provided seven keyword spaces in your Amazon listing, that does not mean that you are limited to only seven words. You can add short Search terms up to 60 characters in each box.

- Consider sentences and phrases that describe or portray the content of your book.

- In the Amazon search bar type in the first word of those sentences and observe the options that the autofill function provides.
- Make a list of these phrases and choose seven for your listing.

Keep the list of the phrases that you don't use for future testing and Amazon Ads.

Exercise seventeen   The Twenty Hooks List
Write twenty separate hooks for your book description.

Remember that your hook is the first words they will see in your book description so craft it well.

Here's a refresher of some of my previous tips when writing your hook:

- Try to complete your hook in around twenty words.
- Don't exceed thirty words.
- For Non-Fiction
    - Start the hook off with a question (address the reader's pain point), why are they looking for your book.
    - Ensure you include a solution to their pain point in the hook. How will your book solve their problem?
- For Fiction paint a picture that will entice the reader into your world. Confirm that your book is taking them where the book cover and title promised.
- Check out your competitor's listings (the top books in your niche or genre).
- Once you have twenty versions of your hook, survey the top three to see which is more appealing to readers. Ask "which description is more likely to get people to buy the book" rather than "which do you like best".

One last point here, you may see that some of the top traditionally published authors don't have well laid out and appealing book descriptions. Their publishers have probably spent a lot of money on marketing and don't feel it's necessary. This is where you have an advantage over them.

THE KEY ELEMENTS FOR (INDIE) AUTHOR SUCCESS

Chapter 8 Pricing and KDP Select

*"Price is what you pay. Value is what you get." – **Warren Buffett***

Product Pricing is about finding the price that the customer is willing to pay but also giving them the value that they perceive they want.

Let's face it if we had an alternative we probably wouldn't pay $1,000 for a new iPhone or Samsung.

The price that you sell your book at is a balancing act between making the most royalties that you can receive and not pricing yourself out of the market.

Your Initial launch price will rarely be the price that you will end up selling your book consistently at, you need to find the sweet spot.

In this chapter, we are going to highlight the key elements of pricing and also any potential impacts on the money that you receive for your book sales.

Phase Pricing
Although I have covered launch schedules in another chapter, I just want to point out that your book may have different prices in the various phases of your launch schedule.

The suggestions for prices in this section are just general examples and you should determine your own price points in relation to your own marketing plans.

Keep a track of where your book is priced in relation to sales, to allow you to find the sweet spot for your sales price and also to help you price future books.

When you publish more than one book in a series you may be considering the first book as being listed permanently for Free, but as this book is aimed at your first book, I am not going to complicate things by going down that rabbit hole.

The different price phases that you may have are:

- The Pre-order price

The Pre-order Price may be lower than the price that you ultimately list your book at on Amazon. This could be as low as $0.99 and is designed to incentivize early buyers.

Remember that pre-order copies don't get their purchases until the day the book goes live (so you miss the opportunity to buy a copy and download it first and check for errors) but it gives your beta readers the chance to get it at a discount as soon as its available. If you send out review copies (rather than have beta readers wait for the book to launch) remember that if they don't purchase a book, their reviews will be unverified, so ensure that they also pre-order a copy of your book.

- The Initial List Price

If you are not using the pre-order function to publish your book your initial list price may be as low as $0.99 as you want initial reviewers to have the chance to buy it cheaper. If you are using the Pre-order function ensure that the initial list price is enough to merit pre-orders.

If your Pre-order price was $0.99 and the initial list price is $1.50, there is little incentive to pre-order the book. Of course, once you are a famous author and readers are clamouring to pre-order your books, you could have both prices the same.

- The Countdown deal
  - If you plan to run a countdown deal, an initial price of $0.99 doesn't give you anywhere to go.
  - The rules for a countdown deal require that you don't have your price lower in the thirty days prior to the deal. A countdown deal for your initial launch means that you can't start at a really low price.
  - If you have a lower price later in your book's life, you should increase your price prior to a countdown deal giveaway as it gives more perceived value for promotions. This is not cheating it is just a marketing tool, and it is usually the list price that I will return to after the launch.
- The Giveaway promotion
  - For the period of your giveaway your price will be $0.00.
  - If you are enrolled in matchbook your discounted price will also be set to $0.00.
- The Post promotion price
  - Once you have finished your promotion you may want to keep your book priced at a low price for a couple of weeks to garner some extra reviews. If you set a high price pre giveaway (or countdown deal), you need to drop the price here.
- The appealing KU price
  - While your book is part of KDP Select it is available free to Kindle Unlimited (KU) members. If your book is listed at only $0.99 it may not seem very appealing to KU Members.
  - Even though a KU reader may have to commit the same amount of time to read your book as a higher priced book there is something in the human psyche that loves a bargain. Knowing that they can read a book priced at $4.99 for Free or a book priced at $0.99 for free can sway the reader's choice.

- The Revised price (post KDPS)
  - If you decide to discontinue the KDPS Programme after a 90 day period, you may choose to lower your price more in line with your competitors.

International Pricing

One of the benefits of a digital product is that there is no real time delay in a reader purchasing your book anywhere on the planet.

When you list your book on the KDP platform it can be distributed on most of Amazon's international sites almost immediately.

When you list your book on KDP you are given the option to manually set the international prices that you will sell your book or tick a box and automatically set the price (based on the current exchange rate of that country's currency to the US Dollar).

The easy option would seem to be to set the prices automatically (as you have the ability to change the prices at any time).

The different levels of income in a country (and thus the expendable income) means that the price that you set can be too low or in most cases, you are pricing your book too high.

A country with a higher income may support a higher price for the same product (your book) but a country with a lower income may require a lower price point for the same product.

I realize that this means that you could gain fewer royalties on each sale but if you are pricing yourself out of the market you are getting no royalties.

There are various ways of calculating the average wages, median incomes and salaries etc of a country.

For the purposes of this comparison we are going to use the average annual wages for 2016 in American dollars:

- United States $60,154
- United Kingdom $42,835
- Australia $52,063
- France $42,992
- Mexico $19,311
- India $14,491
- Kenya $1,600

The purpose of listing the data above is not to debate wages but just to highlight that in different countries the amount of currency that individuals have available to purchase varies.

Case Study — India

If you look at the disparity between India and the United States you can see that the average wage in India is less than 25% of the average wage in the United States.

I am not suggesting that you automatically set your price to 25% in India but asking that you look at the average prices of (the top-selling) books on Amazon.in to give you some guidance when you are listing your books.

The current exchange rate for one US Dollar is approximately ₹65 (Indian Rupee)

The book — Timothy Ferriss's "The 4 Hour Chef":

- Kindle List price on amazon.com = $11.49.
- Kindle List price on Amazon.in = ₹49 (approximately $0.70).
- Hardback List price on amazon.com = $22.57.
- Hardback List price on amazon.in = ₹1190 (approximately $18.30).

At the time of writing this ₹49 is the lowest price that Amazon will allow you to list the kindle version of a book on Amazon.in.

The purpose of this Case study is to give you real data to show you that even a book that is selling lots of copies are adapting their prices to local markets.

Different genres and niches may support slightly higher prices in different markets so I would suggest that you find the average price for books in your area to determine your own list prices.

Pricing of Various Formats

If you are offering multiple versions of your book for sale, the digital version should be cheaper than the print version. Look at the competition but try a few different prices.

If your digital price is close to the print price you may get more paperback sales as they are getting a physical copy for a similar expenditure. Matchbook pricing (as described below) can also help with Paperback sales.

If your reader can get the eBook at a huge discount when they buy the print version of your book and the prices of both versions are similar, it makes sense for them to buy both.

- If you have lots of books you can set your book prices at a selection of price points.
- Don't feel that you are underselling yourself if you have a kindle book listed at $4.99 or less.
- You want to get the book into readers' hands and until you become JK Rowling or Stephen King you may have to have a lower price point in order to gain momentum.
- The type of book and genre will also have some impact on your pricing.
- Non-Fiction books can sell at a higher or lower price than fiction. You need to test the market.

- When you start to publish more books consider selling your books as box sets.
- Pricing boxsets – see Joanna Penn's website "The Creative Penn" (the queen of box sets).

KDP Select

I've included the KDP Select (KDPS) program here because it can have some impacts on the pricing of your book.

When you enrol a book in the KDPS program you are committing to make the digital form of that book available exclusively through KDP.

You commit to KDP select for three months (90 days) at a time and can either choose to commit to another ninety days at the end of each ninety day period. When you enrol a book in KDP there is a tick box to automatically renew your enrolment. If you want to ensure that the three months doesn't accidentally become a six-month exclusivity deal, ensure you untick this box.

You can always tick the box nearer to the end of your ninety days if you want to enrol for another ninety days exclusivity.

Because the ninety days starts from the day you enrol a specific book if you have more than one book published, the enrolment/renewal dates may be different. Ensure you keep a track of these dates.

By enrolling a book in KDPS you are committing to not selling the digital version of that book anywhere else (such as "Smashwords") so why would you do that?

The main reason for new authors to use KDPS is to get their titles some visibility and promotion.

The three main ways this can happen is through:

- Kindle Unlimited.

- Countdown Deals.
- Free Book Giveaways.

Kindle Unlimited (KU)

The Kindle Unlimited service is basically a subscription-based library, like Netflix but instead of paying the monthly fee to watch as many programs as you want, you pay a monthly fee to read the books in the KDPS library.

Each subscriber pays a monthly fee that goes into a financial fund and Amazon distributes part of that fund among the KDPS authors, based on the number of pages of your book that is read.

Amazon uses an algorithm to calculate the Kindle Edition Normalized Page Count (KEPNC), which tends to pay authors around $0.004 - $0.005 per page and this is based on anywhere from 186 to 200 words per page. The way that Amazon estimates page reads has changed a few times already and will no doubt change again.

There is a wide debate on the pros and cons of being part of Kindle Unlimited. In this section I'll provide just an overview of some of those points:

- If you have a 1000 page Kindle book and you are making $9.99 in royalties from that book, you would only get $4.00-$5.00 (based on $0.004-$0.005 a page) if a KU subscriber reads your book instead of purchasing a copy. Here you are potentially losing money on a sale.
- A subscriber to KU has already paid their monthly subscription so they may read your book via the lending library but may not have purchased it for the full price. Here you are reaching an extra reader that you may have missed out on.
- By reading the digital version of your book through KU, the reader may be tempted to purchase a physical copy or audio version of

your book. You have not only reached a reader who might not have purchased the Kindle version of your book at full price, you have potentially upsold to another format of your book.

- The balance between reaching readers and how much each reader is worth is a complex issue.

Countdown Deals

During the ninety days that you are enrolled in the KDPS program, Amazon allows you the ability to run a Countdown deal.

This allows you to set a lower price for your Kindle book and then have it incrementally rise to the current listing price over several days.

Case Study Kindle Countdown

If you have a book currently listed at $4.99:

- You start the countdown deal at $1.99 on Friday and this runs for 24hrs.
- Your next price point (begins as soon as the first 24hrs finishes) is $2.99 on Saturday and this runs for 24hrs.
- Your next price point (begins as soon as the second 24hrs finishes) is $3.99 on Sunday and this runs for 24hrs.
- Monday your listing price returns to $4.99.

Summary based on a Countdown deal set to run from 7.00 A.M.			
Day	Time	Price	Remarks
Thursday	7.00 AM	$4.99	Initial List Price
Friday	7.00 AM	$1.99	
Saturday	7.00 AM	$2.99	
Sunday	7.00 AM	$3.99	
Monday	7.00 AM	$4.99	Back to initial list price

The benefits of a countdown deal promotion:

- You are creating a sense of urgency as the current price, the discount price and the time remaining for the promotion (as a countdown clock) are all displayed on the books details page.
- Amazon provides a dedicated website http://Amazon.com/kindlecountdowndeals where customers can find your deal.
- Although you are discounting the price you are not giving the book away free (so you are still receiving some royalties).
- Even on the countdown days that your book is listed below the $2.99 threshold (for the 70% royalties), if it is normally listed at $2.99, your book still qualifies for 70% royalties on those days.
- Your KDP report lists the total sales at each of the discounted prices compared to the normal list price. This can help you find the optimal price point for your book.

Free Book Giveaways
During each of the ninety-day periods that you are enrolled in KDPS, Amazon allows you book giveaways.

As an alternative to the countdown deal, you can list your book in five days of free book giveaways.

You can choose to spread these days out and list the giveaways one day at a time or batch all of the days together and launch a five-day giveaway altogether.

The purpose of your giveaway is to increase exposure to your book and hopefully receive some positive reviews on your listing.

As no one likes being the first to read a book it is important that you have some reviews before launching a giveaway.

Even though a reader is not paying a financial price for your book, they are committing their time to read it so they want to see that it will be worth their time.

As I have stated in the review chapter of this book, you should aim for at least ten reviews by the time of your promotion.

When you list your promo on some websites that require a minimum number of reviews, they will check for the reviews when you list your promo not the day of the promo. Ensure you already have those reviews on your listing before trying to list your promotion on those sites.

I've actually found paid book sales can increase a few weeks after a giveaway rather than straight away. This can be down to not having a sufficient launch promotion.

When Amazon first launched the giveaway option, the sales counted to your books overall BSR. Now that Amazon treats the paid ranking and free ranking differently, your free downloads will not count towards your listing.

One advantage of a free giveaway is that even though you book is free, a download during a giveaway is actually classed as a Verified sale.

Taxes
A quick note on tax (as I live outside the USA).

Although income isn't the only measure of successful publishing, like any business venture, the balance sheet is important.

When you start selling your books on Amazon.com the royalties you receive are classed as income. This income can be liable for taxes (up to 30%), which Amazon withhold automatically.

If you are a Non-US resident you may be able to reduce the amount of taxes that amazon withhold. There are several factors involved here, including whether or not your country of residence has a reciprocal tax agreement with the US.

Because taxes are an individual issue and there are so many permutations that even a stand-alone book wouldn't cover all eventualities, I just want to raise awareness in this section.

Assess your own situation and ensure that whatever taxes are being applied to your royalties are correct.

If you can reduce the amount from 30% to 5% (which in some cases you may be able to), that's quite a difference.

I applied for an American Employer Identification Number (EIN) when I started as an Amazon product seller, this meant that I already had an EIN and made the process easier.

We sometimes get distracted at the start of our publishing journey, then we sell more books and then life can get in the way. Ensure that you set your accounts up correctly the first time.

If you need to seek professional tax advice please do but ensure that your KDP accounts are set up correctly.

The KDP Dashboard

When you first start making book sales the Dashboard on your KDP account can seem confusing.

Personally tracking my daily book sales on a spreadsheet for over 18 months, it never seemed to make much sense.

The Pending US revenue in my reports is rarely the same on a daily basis. The value increasing I understood but some days the figure goes up and some days it goes down.

You can download detailed reports to drill down into the finer details of your sales but if you just want to see an overview of sales and pages read, I recommend "Book Report".

If you go to the site https://www.getbookreport.com it allows you to add this free tool to your Browser Bookmarks Bar. Once you've installed book report it allows you to generate a display (when you are logged into your KDP dashboard) that makes it much easier to understand how your books are performing.

Affiliate Associates and Affiliate links

Although the Associate program may not seem to be directly linked to your books price, by being part of the Amazon Associate program you can earn a royalty when you promote a product on Amazon that a customer buys.

Remember that your book is a product so you can get an affiliate payment on top of your royalties (for the same purchase).

The way this works is that you create a hyperlink to a product (that is linked to your associate account) and if customers click on the link and then purchase that item you receive a fee of between 4% and 10% depending on the item.

The current program doesn't just refer to your book sales, if a customer clicks on your link and purchases your book and then buys other digital products within a 24 hour period, you can get royalties on those purchases too. Amazon rewards you for bringing them customers.

You can advertise these links on your website, and in other promotional ways.

If you have a website you may already have links to physical products on your site but have you got affiliate links to your books on your site?

If you have affiliate links to your books you can earn extra income on top of your royalties from the sale of your own book.

You can also place these affiliate links in the back of your Kindle books (in your section on "other books by this author").

 If you can get an extra 4% (or more payment) from your book, why wouldn't you?

If no one buys anything from your link within 180 days you may have to resubmit to the program but if your books are a business, you want to optimize profits.

N.B. The Associate program is not available in all countries. If Amazon's history has anything to teach us, they are constantly tweaking their terms and royalty or affiliate percentages aren't set in stone. Always monitor your book's income and take that into account with your book pricing strategy.

KDP Pricing Tab

As the "KDP eBook Price" tab is one of the key tools to publishing your book through KDP I have laid out the information here as per the tab (with explanations) so that you can become comfortable with its use.

When you are ready to upload your book to KDP feel free to return to this section and use it as a guide.

KDP Select enrolment

KDP select is an agreement to distribute the eBook format of your book exclusively through KDP for ninety days. You can enrol all or none of your books individually in this service. You can choose to set it to automatically renew your subscription to KDPS every 90 days or choose to set it to manually renew (if you set it to manual renewal it can be easy to forget to renew). You can join or re-join KDPS at any time.

Territories

As an indie author producing a unique piece of work (your own new book), you should own the distribution rights to all territories.

This section of the tab was primarily for traditional publishers. When you enter into a contract with a publisher you can usually agree to lease them the license to the distribution of your book (the rights) either worldwide or in individual territories.

If an author wants to distribute their book through KDP but they have still licensed to distribute their book in various territories, they would have to choose the territories that they still own the distribution rights for.

For Indie Authors it's not usually an issue but something to bear in mind if you ever publish through a traditional publisher.

Royalty and Pricing

Although there are some restrictions on the amount of royalties that you will receive, remember that as an Indie author, you are the owner of the book and can choose what price to sell it at.

- KDP price support

This is a function that is currently in Beta (trial) format. Amazon analyses data from similar books to yours and suggests the list price that should bring you the maximum royalties on your book. I ran it through one of my books and it suggested that similar books priced at $3.49 had produced the highest earnings at this list price (based on 70% royalties). You might want to consider this information as part of your pricing strategy but I'd caution against solely using this information to set your price.

- Select a royalty plan

If your book is priced above the threshold in the Primary marketplace (e.g. $2.99 on Amazon.com) it can qualify for 70% royalties. Below this threshold, you fall into the 30% royalty band.

- Marketplaces

As we discussed in the case study you can choose to individually adjust the list price of your book in the various Amazon Countries.

There are certain caveats to qualifying for 70% royalties. For some territories, you must be enrolled in KDP select to benefit from 70% royalties (even if you exceed the price threshold). Don't assume that at a certain price you will receive a specific royalty percentage, regularly review the different marketplaces.

Matchbook
The Matchbook price is a discounted price that you can choose to allow Purchasers of your paperback to pay for the digital version at the time of purchase.

You can set the Matchbook price to $2.99, $1.99, $0.99 or Free.

This can help promote paperback sales but also increase your royalties by inducing book buyers to buy more than one format of the same book.

Here's an example of how it works

- Your book is normally listed on amazon.com at $8.77 for the Kindle Version and $14.99 for the paperback version.
- You set the Matchbook Price at $2.99
- When a customer buys the Paperback for $14.99, they are given the option to purchase the Kindle version of the same book at a discount of almost $6 ($8.77-$2.99).
- This is a great deal for the customer and some extra royalties for you.

As an extra incentive for this, Amazon waives the normal $2.99 threshold for (70%) Royalties on this transaction. If your Matchbook price is only $1.99 but the Kindle version is normally above the 70% threshold, you get 70% royalties on the $1.99 Sale.

Book Lending

This setting allows buyers of your book to lend it to other members of their family (through Amazon) for up to 14 days. If your royalties are set to 70% enrolment, this facility is compulsory. Some people may be concerned that they are missing out on royalties but I view it that people borrow print books from my bookshelf at home all of the time. This is just extra exposure and if your book is a Non-Fiction Guide (like this book), they may decide to buy it after the 14 day period.

Terms & Conditions

There is a link in this section (of the KDP site) to the latest Amazon terms and conditions. These are the rules that you are agreeing to abide by when you publish your book on Kindle.

This section is situated here because it is confirming that you agree to Amazons Terms when you take the next step and click on the "Publish your Kindle eBook" button.

Although your only choice is to agree to the terms or not to publish on KDP, I do suggest that you read these terms before you publish and on a periodic basis.

There are lots of Terms in there to take on board:

- It is your responsibility to keep yourself familiarised when these Terms are updated. When they are updated you have the choice to keep, publishing under the new Terms or withdraw your books. They do email you when they update the terms but with our busy lives (and ongoing software updates), I find few people read updates to Terms and conditions.

- Pricing and conversion rates for various currencies etc.

The main thing to note (unless they change their Terms) is that they are basically distributing a product for you. You are not handing over your licensing rights to publish in specific regions and (except when you are subscribed to KDP Select) if you want to distribute your works on other platforms it is up to you.

Bear in mind that Amazon accounts for between 50-80% of digital book sales so the Pros of selling under their Terms should outweigh the Cons that they make all of the rules.

Great on Kindle
At the time of writing this book, Amazon is beta testing a 50% royalty option called "Great on Kindle". This is primarily aimed at books over $10. Whereas previously your royalties have been limited when the list price of your Kindle book was over $10, this has the potential to pay you more royalties.

I mention this option only to make you aware that Amazon will no doubt change royalty pay out options in the future. As Amazon has cornered such a large section of the world's book sales, they have the power to reduce the amount of royalties that they pay authors. Wider distribution of your book should be part of your long-term plan.

Exercises
As you come closer to your book launch you will have a multitude of activities to undertake, so I offer you these exercises as preparation and to save you some time later.

Exercise Eighteen   Pick a Comparative Listing Price
Choose 6 similar books to your books, length, and subject matter notoriety (don't choose a best seller in your niche/genre).

Aim for books with a BSR from 30,000 to 50,000.

To ensure that you are comparing books at a similar level ensure that they are similar in the following aspects:

- The number of pages.
- The number of reviews.
- How long the book has been published.
- How many formats the book is available in.

Choose a comparative price for your books list price.

Exercise Nineteen   Determine the Price Stages of Your Book
You can change your list prices at any time but here are a few suggestions for some of your price points:

- The Pre-order price — if you intend to use this KDP function, you may choose to make the price difference between this and the initial list price attractive.
- Your initial list— if you aren't using Pre-orders remember that this may be quite low (to get some early reviews).
- The Post promotion price — prior to the Countdown Deals you are not allowed to have a lower price for the previous thirty days. For an initial launch countdown deal, you may have started your listing at a higher price point. For subsequent countdown deals in the future, you may decide to increase your price to $3.99 or $4.99.
- The Appealing Kindle Unlimited (KU) price — remember that you want to optimize your book value to KU readers. If you decide to subscribe to KDPS at a later date you may want to revise your list price first.

Exercise Twenty   Install Book Report
Once your book has gone live on KDP, login to https://www.getbookreport.com and install the Book Report tool to your Bookmarks Bar

I have no affiliation with this site and this exercise is just a suggestion to help you understand the reports on your KDP account.

Exercise Twenty One   Setup your Amazon Associate Account

If you haven't set up your website yet, then come back to this later but:

- Ensure that you have affiliate links to your books on your website.
- Ensure that you put affiliate links to your other books in your published books.

If you don't have a website you can't currently join this program but as an author aiming to maximize income, I suggest you may want to do this.

Chapter 9 Author Central and Media Packs

"History will be kind to me for I intend to write it." — ***Winston Churchill***

One of the key elements of publishing success is to build a relationship and integrity with your readers. Although a lot of authors are introverts, the idiosyncrasies of the digital world mean that you can shelter behind a digital screen whilst achieving exposure on a global scale.

Remember that by publishing a book you are opening yourself up to some scrutiny by the universe so some exposure is just part and parcel of the publishing process.

As an author publishing on Amazon through KDP, you are provided the opportunity of your own (author Central) home page on their platform.

I am not suggesting that this is a replacement for your website or any other promotion tools that you have. It just makes sense to make the most of a conduit directly to your readers that is provided for free and is situated in one of the biggest bookstores in the world.

Your Author Central Page:
It can take three to five days for your Author Page to appear on Amazon but as you can start to add content as soon as it is setup, don't delay.

Manage your Biography (Bio)

This is the time to shine and tell the readers what you want them to know about you. Lots of authors can see themselves as introverts and feel that their Bio is self-publicizing.

- As an author, you need to let people know about you. I want you to be successful so please (even if you feel you are only doing this for me), embrace your Biography and promote yourself.
- Before you go out and start typing straight into your author central Bio, take some time to prepare it. Type it into whatever word processing software you use and then copy and paste it.
- Better to delay uploading it so that your first impression provides some semblance of professionalism. Although don't use this as an excuse to procrastinate and wait for perfection though.
- Use your words wisely. Remember that as an author you have a lot of words inside you.

Updates to Bios can appear in less than 30 minutes, so ensure that you use the preview option before you save any changes.

Upload Photos

Remember that the purpose of uploading a photo is to help personalize yourself with the readers SO SHOW YOUR FACE!

- You can upload multiple photos and although the default of the system categorizes the photo most recently uploaded as the primary (the one that customers see on the author page) you can reorder the photos quickly, using the "manage" function.
- I realize that it might seem easier to just redirect readers to your own website (or any other external page) but I personally prefer to see a face rather than an avatar on Amazon.
- In an era where people are discouraged from engaging if they need to click twice in an online system (rather than just once), you want to encourage people to click on your Author Central page.

- The whole point of optimizing your Author central page is to maximize engagement and readers like me will be less likely to click without a picture. The lack of a photo of the Authors face makes it seem that the info is not directly available.
- Although you may not have the funds to initially pay for professional photos, please ensure that your pictures are of a reasonable quality. It's amazing the quality of pictures that today's smartphones can produce.

Author Central specifies the technical specifications for these images so ensure that you adhere to their standards.

Manage Blog Feeds
Although you may see your author central as a static display, it does provide you the ability to make it more dynamic.

- I empathize with the concern that the more places that you display information, the more places you need to update.
- If you have a blog, Author central allows you an automatic update here.
- Bloggers will know how to easy it is to link your blog feed here. This means that blog teasers will automatically be updated when you leave new posts on your blog.

Readers can choose to follow your Amazon profile and be made aware of your updates but adding your blog feed can also peak readers interest and get them to view your website.

Upload Videos
The ability to upload videos is yet another way of promoting you, your brand and your books.

- Owing to amazons proclivity to stop you taking their customers away from amazons website there are certain restrictions on content (see Amazons up to date terms before uploading a video).

- You can still provide a video for a book or just a little intro about who you are.
- Although you can't link to external videos such as your Youtube site, this is yet another extra opportunity to market yourself.
- You can add up to eight videos and determine the order that they appear on your Amazon author page. If you are uploading a video for each book, why not have your most recent book showing first?

You want to ensure that your videos are of a good quality and there are certain specifications for these images:

- The videos currently need to be one of the following formats avi, wmv, flv, mov or mpg.
- No more than 10mins in length.
- It can take up to 24hrs to be processed (and then you must press "approve video" to make it live).
- As the still of the video (displayed on by default on Amazon) is randomly chosen from the beginning of the video, ensure that the first few seconds of your video are an appropriate video. Ideally a still of your smiling face or your book cover.

Manage Events
As this book is a beginner's guide, you may not be at a stage of your publishing journey to have a book signing or other literary events to list.

- Like all of the features that are available for your Amazon Authors page, use them as soon as you can.

Create an Author Page URL
A Uniform Resource Identifier (URL) is an easily shareable link that you can use to direct readers straight to your author page.

- By creating a link you can add it to your email signature block, social media posts and any other digital promotions.

- This is again another way of solidifying your brand and linking your information together.

Manage Your Bibliography
Upload book images

- If your books are listed on Amazon you shouldn't need to add additional images.
- Although this area of author central only displays one image for each book, you can still check that all formats of the book are linked. Just clicking on the books tab when you are logged in to author central, allows you to confirm this.

Manage Editorial Reviews
- In this section, you can copy reviews from blog sites or print media.
- It is just another way to allow you to enhance your appeal to the reader.

Author Central Checklist
- Is your Bio up to date?
- Have you uploaded (up to date) profile pictures showing your face?
- Have you uploaded at least one video?
- Is your blogs RS feed linked to your profile?
- Are all of your current books listed in your bibliography?
- If you have any editorial reviews are they listed here?

Media Packs
Some People refer to an author's Media Pack as your Press kit because it is useful to have your information consolidated in preparation for interviews or book promotions. Although it can be useful to have your information prepared in advance of interviews,

the main reason to compile a media pack is to maximize your exposure.

Biographies (Bios)

As an author, you will usually have your Bio in more locations than just your Amazon Author Central page. The longer you are an author the wider you will distribute your Bio and the harder it is to ensure that all of the Bios are kept up to date.

Historically authors used to have a Bio on the back of their print books. As this has predominantly been replaced by "about the author" sections in most books, it can be updated without having to replace the book cover.

Having multiple Bio's out in the digital universe can be difficult to keep track of. Although minor updates may not require you to replace all of your Bios, the most efficient way to ensure uniformity is to keep a record of their locations.

I keep a copy of all of my Bios in a folder labelled with a Bio number and the date (e.g. Bio No1Dtd260116).

Some Information I include in my Bio tracker:

- The Bio number.
- The Location of Each Bio.
- A link to each Bio's location.
- The date that the Bio was created (if a Bio is published in a book I use the books first publication date).
- The date that the Bio was last updated.
- The length of the Bio (Different types of promotion require different size Bios so it can be useful to know how many words a bio contains).

Sample Questions and Answers

As your author profile grows you may find that certain questions will crop up repeatedly and having a list of these questions (with answers at the ready) can reduce your requirement for following up with interviewers. Knowing what you have said in the past can also maintain a uniform profile.

A few of the type of questions that you might want to include are:

- What was your inspiration for each book (or series)?
- Which authors inspired you growing up?
- When did you first start to write?
- What inspired you to start writing?
- Who do you see as your audience for each book (or series)?

Images
It is useful to have a set of images for your books and for you.

Keeping a folder with an up to date image of each of your books front covers will allow you to save time when you are promoting specific books.

Just as you should have pictures on your Author Central Profile, you should keep a selection of photos of yourself in your media pack. Some promotions require headshots and different social media platforms can require that images adhere to different specifications.

Your publishing career may stretch for many years (in fact copyright means that your books will outlast your lifetime) so ensure that you regularly update your profile pictures.

Book Links
Keeping a list of links to each of your books as part of your media pack will allow you to save time when you are promoting specific books.

This has several benefits when your links are included in promotions:

- For books with a wider distribution, you can appeal to readers who prefer buying through iTunes or Kobo (etc.) rather than Amazon.
- If your links are used to purchase your books, you can earn extra money through the likes of Amazon's affiliate program.

A List of All of Your Contact Details
Most authors will have at least one website and potentially several email addresses.

Today the social media platform that is in vogue may be Twitter and tomorrow it could be something that is as yet unheard of.

Ensure that all of your social media handles are included in your media pack and as your profile grows, remember to update this information.

You may use different emails for business contact (e.g. reporter contact) and have some emails linked to your website. Ensure that you list the correct contact details for promotions and do not list personal contact details in your media pack that you don't wish to be shared.

Exercises
Your Media pack will change through time but the sooner you start to compile it, the better prepared you will be for marketing.

Exercise Twenty Two   Have a Good Quality Picture Taken of Yourself
Ideally, you want to provide continuity so you will likely be using the same image of yourself in various places.

Points to bear in mind:

- With the availability and quality of cameras on our smartphones, we should all be able to get great pictures but ensure that they are of a good quality.
- It's surprising how inexpensive it can be for a couple of pictures but if Cashflow is an issue there are less expensive ways to get quality pictures.

Contact tutors at your local college or high school, their students may be glad of the experience (and should have access to modern equipment).

Exercise Twenty Three   Write Two Versions of Your Bio
Have a couple of versions of your bio available. For most marketing or promotional sites, they will want information about you. As they may have limited space for your information, you may need to abridge your initial bio.

Don't change the information that your bio contains, as you are still targeting the same market.

For this exercise just produce a long and short version of your bio.

- Create one Bio 400 words long.
- Create one Bio 800 words long.

By having two different lengths of your bio readily available, you can quickly adapt them to meet future requirements.

Exercise Twenty Four   Write a Book synopsis
Having a synopsis for your book available in various lengths will save you time later. As with your bio, marketing activities may provide limited space for your book synopsis.

For this exercise produce three versions of the synopsis for the same book.

- Create one synopsis 100 words long.

- Create one synopsis 200 words long.
- Create one synopsis 300 words long.

This exercise provides you with three versions of your synopsis but can also help with the formulation of the description for your book listing.

Chapter 10   Reviews the Holy Grail

"I didn't read reviews earlier in my career, but I read them now as I'm older. I read them all." — **Steven Spielberg**

Reviews are the lifeblood of your book on Amazon

Reviews are the lifeblood of product sellers on Amazon and this is just as true for Amazon booksellers.

Amazon has designed their algorithm to put products in front of their customers that they are most likely to want to buy. Product reviews are a factor in the algorithms calculation but also a psychological factor in customer purchasing.

The majority of humans prefer not to be the first to try something. If they see that a product has no reviews they perceive that they are one of the first customers and are less likely to buy.

If you want to sell books on Amazon, you are going to need book reviews.

Let me begin by saying that there is no one magic bullet for getting book reviews, you need to see activities designed to get reviews for what they are, marketing activities.

What Should a Reviewer Write

Although you should not be writing reviews for your readers to post, lots of readers don't leave a review because they don't know what to write.

The main point of a review is to help prospective readers decide if the book is for them.

Whenever a reader asks me what to write in a review, I suggest that they just need to write a few lines.

If they ask for more guidance I suggest that they consider some or all of the points below:

- What did they like about the book?
- Did the book remind them of any other authors (and to name at least one of those authors)?
- Did the book remind them of any other books (and to name at least one of those books)?
- How was it similar or different to other books/authors?

I personally think that these tips help the reviewer and also anyone reading the review.

It's A Numbers Game

Whatever process or strategy you adopt to get more reviews for your book, it's a numbers game. Results will vary but from my own experience and those of fellow authors (I communicate with) the average number of book buyers that actually leave a review for the book is somewhere between 0.5% to 2.5%

Personally, I'd say that the 2.5% may be a bit on the high side, so whatever you can do to increase the conversion rate from reader to reviewer should be considered.

Mindset

When you start to view reviews as one of your biggest marketing tools, you are getting yourself into the right mindset.

Like all marketing activities, the stage of your books life cycle will determine which activities you carry out at that time.

Some of the marketing techniques will garner immediate reviews, some future reviews and some no reviews at all. By utilizing multiple techniques you are giving yourself a better chance of getting reviews (and ultimately sales).

A lot of authors see themselves as introverts and feel uncomfortable asking for reviews.

As an author, you are expecting your words to be read and you have the benefits of your writing skills. Embrace those skills and use them to your benefit. By asking for reviews in writing even introverts can ask for reviews.

Are you Famous

If you have a huge fan base (such as Stephen King or Dan Brown) who are waiting eagerly for your next book to launch, your initial book sales may not need a pile of reviews to make them happen.

Unfortunately for the rest of us mere mortals, Amazon reviews are one of the key marketing elements (and lifeblood of our Amazon book sales).

You might not have your book cover decided yet and may just have a working title, but if you haven't already got a system set up for getting book reviews it's time to think about this prickly subject.

Before we go any further in this chapter I need to be honest with you and tell you that you will need to invest some of your budget in getting reviews.

You will definitely need to invest some of your time and there may be some requirement for financial investment. It's true that you can accrue reviews with no financial investment but there will be certain times where even a small financial investment makes sense.

Activities and Results

Although there are many activities that you can carry out to promote Reviews I like to divide them into two categories:

- Seed Activities: As we discovered earlier in the book a seed activity is something that you need to do in order to produce a result in the future. In this section, we are considering seed activities to obtain a review but those reviews may not eventuate for some time in the future (sometimes months in the future).

- Immediate Activities: An immediate activity is something that can produce a review of your book as soon as your book goes live or within the first thirty days of the activity.

Seed Activities

I know that you probably want to skip ahead to the immediate activities but by definition, you need to plant a seed before it will grow.

Building your mailing lists

In an earlier chapter, we talked about starting your email list.

As I stated above, having a fan base waiting eagerly for your next book is a great way to get some initial sales. In order to build this fan base you need to build your list and in order to get people to part with their email addresses (and subscribe to your list), you need to provide something of value.

Just as with the other chapters in this book, two I am not going to fill this chapter with all of the mechanics of list building (such as autoresponders etc.) as there is a whole industry dedicated, just for list building.

I have listed this option first in this chapter because as you build your following it can create a longevity for future reviews. One way of directing readers to your list is by having a link in your Kindle book.

That link will need a compelling reason for the reader to click on it (such as an offer for a free resource) but it is a way of using the contents of your book to build your list. As the reader has already bought the book with the link inside, you are growing potential readers for future books here.

As we saw earlier in the book, If you write in different niches/genres it is important to determine if you need separate mailing lists for each of them. Although there may be some readers who will read your work in each of the genres it is better that they are in a separate email list for each.

When I first started writing I was not aware of this opportunity and wasted a good amount of time that I could have been building a list. I was fortunate that I built a free online course and later added the link to it in one of my books as an afterthought. This started a list for me almost by accident.

Building your website
Building a website (or having one built) doesn't have to be your first activity. I have included it here as it can be an integral part of increasing your visibility and building your email list.

There are a lot of benefits to having a website as an author.

As well as a repository that you can direct readers to (for the promotion of your other books/products) and a place to post your book affiliate links, there are some benefits of having your own website relating to Reviews.

- Websites such as the Indieview.com require you to have a link to their site (on your website) to be on their reviewer list.
- You can run competitions and other promotions on your own site to tempt reviews.

Advanced Review Copies ARC's

We covered ARC's in some detail in the chapter on book launches but I just want to emphasize here that you can distribute ARCs to potential reviewers. If a reader places a review based on the fact that they received a review copy (and doesn't purchase a copy of your book through Amazon) the Review will be classed as unverified. If you sell physical copies of your book at book signings or other channels, the reviews they garner will also not be verified.

Although an unverified review can be just as genuine as a verified review, the Amazon algorithm doesn't look at them the same. Remember that the Amazon algorithm was designed to benefit Amazon readers, so it looks at a review on a copy of a book Amazon sells, differently to a review on a copy it hasn't sold.

ARC copies can solicit reviews but they can require a follow up. We are all busy so even a free book copy doesn't guarantee a review.

Subscribing to Forums and Facebook groups

As we discussed earlier in this book, before you post on a forum, in a Facebook group or contact a member directly you need to have built up some social currency. By being an active member of a group or forum it will give you some credibility (social currency). Don't be that person who joins a group and starts to spam everyone from day one. Social currency is about relationship building on social networks.

Ensure that you join groups that are relevant to you. A group full of romance book authors may not be the ideal audience for your books on quantum mechanics etc.

A couple of useful groups:

- K boards forums
- Facebook groups

Library sites:

- Goodreads

- Librarything.com

You need to build a profile on some of these sites. For Librarything.com you need to have ranked 50 books in your profile in order to promote a giveaway

I am fortunate that I am a speed reader and when I signed up for Librarything I already had about 100 books on my Goodreads profile. It still took me a while to mirror this info but I was basically just copying the info I had already created on one site to another.

Simplify the Review Process
As an indie author myself, I know the importance of reviews but even I don't review every book I read.

When we look at a service like UBER it benefits the driver and the passenger to rate their journey. The system is set up this way.

The Amazon platform is skewed so that there is not much incentive for buyers to leave reviews, even though they are important for authors and sellers (it is important that you make it as easy as possible for readers to leave a review).

With our ever-diminishing attention span, statistics show that where someone has to click twice to make a purchase or navigate elsewhere online (that second click is enough that), they are more likely to abandon the journey.

Basically, humans are getting lazier!

Getting readers to log in to Amazon and find their order to place a review can seem like too much trouble for even the most ardent fan. Doesn't it make sense to have a link that they can click on while reading your book and go straight to that books review page?

One of the benefits that a Kindle book has over a physical product is that you can actually ask nicely for a review within the book (product) and create a link directly to your books review page.

Remember that the purpose of this link is to make it easier for readers to leave a review.

- Leaving a message saying something like "if you liked this book please feel free to leave a review, so that I can benefit other readers with my next book" might encourage reviews but it is still a bit passive. Ensure that you include the link.
- You need to be careful with your terminology as if Amazon believe that you are breaking their terms of service they will stop you selling on their platform.

When to create the review link

Until your book listing is live on Amazon you will not be able to access its review page. This means that you will need to add the link and upload an updated version of your book ASAP.

If you have managed to upload a manuscript and get your book live, you should have no issues uploading your updated manuscript.

As some new authors worry about making any changes to a book once it's live, I have provided a simple overview of the process in the section (uploading your revised content) below.

Where do you get the link

Although you can create a link on a specific Amazon site (such as Amazon.com), that link will usually not work on the other Amazon sites that you book is listed (such as Amazon.co.uk).

- One of the easiest ways to create a universal link is to use one of the free online tools to do it for you.
- I recommend Russell Phillip's UK Book website Russellphillipsbooks.co.uk. In the tools section of his website, he has a review link generation tool.
- You simply type in the ASIN of your book and it creates a link that you can cut and paste into your book or anywhere else that you may be posting review requests. Don't worry if you are outside

the United Kingdom, the link may include UK in the title but it is a universal link.

Creating a HyperLink

Here's an example of a link that I created for one of my books (using this tool):

- The book is called "How to Choose a Writing Coach" and the ASIN is B076VFB3C3
- The Link that is created is in this format https://www.rpbook.co.uk/azr/B076VFB3C3
- Rather than leave it in this format, I typed the following text in my book: "To leave a Review for How to Choose a Writing Coach please click here" and insert a hyperlink.

Using the text with a hyperlink looks more professional and avoids confusion for international readers (as they don't see the words ".co.uk"). This also means that I can type, the text in my initial manuscript and when I want to upload an updated manuscript I can insert a hyperlink without changing the text.

For anyone that hasn't used a hyperlink before most Word processing software such as MS Word has a similar process:

- Highlight the Text that you want to include in the link. In my example I highlighted "click here" (in "To leave a Review for How to Choose a Writing Coach please click here").
- Click on the option to insert hyperlink.
- Copy and paste the link into the space provided (in my case that was https://www.rpbook.co.uk/azr/B076VFB3C3).
- Click Ok and the text now has a hyperlink attached to the books review page on the reader's local Amazon Platform.

Where to place the link

Placement of your suggestion for a review is important.

- Don't put it on page one as they will want to read your book before leaving a review (and they will forget your request start once they have read the book).
- Don't put it right at the back after the glossary or index (or it may never be seen).

Having a thank you page for a reader (listed in the contents) especially when a book is about self-development or positivity means that you are engaging a reader and making them feel positive. If they are in a positive state of mind, it may help your review.

- For non-fiction books, the reader is reading it to get something out of it (for an autobiography it may just be an inspiration) so if they are reading a book thinking what's in it for me, a feel-good page makes sense.
- We aren't trying to con the reader or play Jedi mind tricks on them, just optimizing their incentives to leave a review.

Uploading Your Revised Content
If you have followed the steps above, the only revision to your manuscript is the addition of the hyperlink. Remember to save your updated manuscript under a different file name so if there are any issues you can always reload the manuscript that you know works.

To upload your new manuscript go to the bookshelf section of your KDP Account.

- To the right-hand side of "Kindle book actions" click on the box with the three buttons …
- From the options Select "Edit E book content"
- Click on the button marked "Upload eBook manuscript" and select your updated manuscript file (complete with the review link).

If you really want you can go through the Preview process (using "launch previewer") but if you have only added a hyperlink you can press the "save and continue" button.

- The process will take you to the "Kindle eBook Pricing" tab. As you are changing nothing here just press the button marked "Publish Your Kindle eBook".
- You will get an email once the updated version of your book is available on Amazon.
- Once you know the new version is available, check the "look inside" function to ensure that there are no issues (and that the link works).

Contests

Using Twitter, Facebook Ads, Goodreads Giveaways or other online contests, you can raise the profile of your book. Although there is no guarantee that winning contestants won't just sell your book on eBay rather than reading and reviewing it, you are increasing your visibility.

Amazon Giveaways and Countdown deals

If your books are enrolled in the KDP Select program you have the opportunity to utilize the free giveaway days or the countdown deals.

The premise behind these two options is that you are giving your eBooks away at a discount (or for free) in the hope that the reader will be so grateful that they will leave you a review.

The fact that you use either of these options is not a guarantee of reviews, both of these options are just, in fact, a form of "Sale" and need to be promoted.

Think how much time Amazon spend on promoting events such as their Black Friday Sales.

Those huge events have lots of exposure and as they are annual events there is a built-in audience already waiting for them.

Here are some key points to take into account when using these options.

- This is a numbers game. If you are fortunate to have one thousand or more downloads during your promotion, it may still only result in ten reviews or less.
- If it is a numbers game then you want to get as many of your books read at once.
- Because a book is free it may get downloaded (along with a lot of other free eBooks by the same person) and never get read.
- If you list your book at $0.99 (even though you may have fewer copies downloads), it can make readers more likely to read as they have actually paid something for the book.
- You want to make it as easy as possible for readers to leave a review. As we mentioned above, once your book is live on Amazon you can copy a link to the review page of your book and paste it into your eBook then update this updated copy. Ensure this link is in your book before your promotion.
- Nobody wants to be the first to download a book so ensure that you get ten to twenty reviews prior to your promotion. You may think you are giving readers a present but if they are committing time to read a book, they want to perceive value in the book.
- Limit the frequency that you use these options for each book. For each 90 day enrolment, Amazon allows you the same amount of days for giveaway or countdown deals. It is recommended that you only use these options once every six months per book.

N.B. Results from promotions may not be apparent right away. If your book includes a program spanning a set amount of time (e.g. a 21 day plan) then you may not get any reviews until the end of that period.

Promotion Sites

When you run the promotions you want to get the most downloads of your book. There are lots of promotion sites out there that are dedicated to promoting discount or free books to their subscribers.

The people running these sites may love books but ultimately they are in business. Some of the sites (such as bookbub.com) charge a hefty fee to promote and others allow you to list your promotion for free. In an effort to maintain their subscribers, most sites will have certain criteria for books to be submitted to their sites.

You are going to want to submit your promotions to as many sites as possible and in order to do this, you will need to do some preparation in advance.

I have covered this in more detail in the chapter on launches but some important things to bear in mind are:

- Some sites require a minimum of ten reviews (at least half of them verified) before they will allow you to post your promotion on their site.
- Some of these sites may offer a free option (that is not guaranteed to be shown) or a guaranteed listing for between $5 and $15. Even if your budget is tight, I advise you not to waste over half an hour completing and inputting lots of data for a promo into a site that may not promote your book when you could guarantee promotion for as little as $5.
- Some of the more established sites will have a larger number of subscribers so you may choose to promote on those sites. Larger sites may cover multiple genres and they may not promote your book to all of these genres so take that into account.
- Some of the newer sites are looking for content. They may not have as many subscribers yet but try a few as they may have fresh avenues for their promotions

In the resources section at the back of this book, I have listed some suggested promotional sites.

Author Central
Your author central page is supplied for free.

I go into this element in more depth in another chapter but I List this as an option to list your promotion. If a reader is looking at your profile on your author central page, you have obviously peaked their interest. Whilst you have a captive audience it would be rude not to tell them about your upcoming promotions.

Links and ongoing reviews
Ensure that all of your books have links to your other books in the back of your eBook.
Ensure that all of your books have a section in the back thanking the reader and suggesting that they can place a review.

Immediate Activities
Promoting to your Mailing List
Once you have built your mailing list you can convert some of this list into beta readers and get them to read the book before your listing goes live. This means that they are ready to provide reviews immediately your book does go live.

Promoting in Forums and Facebook groups
Having built some social currency in a group (or forum) you may feel excited and you want to share your latest promotion. STOP RIGHT THERE! CURB YOUR ENTHUSIASM!

I know that you are excited but trust me when I say that you need to take a breath. I've been there and blasted out my free giveaway (I'm doing them a favour right?) and upset site admins/moderators.

For the rest of this section please assume that the word group covers both a group and a forum.

Please consider these points before posting:

- Have you really been an active member of this group? This doesn't just mean posting about yourself but actually providing benefits/support for other group members.
- Do you know the rules of the group? If you are unsure it's always respectful to contact an administrator /moderator before posting.
- Once you are sure that your posting will be within the rules, make your posting respectful and provide as much benefit to the group as possible.
- Ensure that you triple check your posting for mistakes and ensure that the post highlights the benefits for the reader.
- Ensure that this promotion is relevant to this group. Because inducing reviews is a numbers game, we may feel that just getting our information out to the most people is the goal of a promotion. The goal is actually to get it to the right people. If you post a promotion for a romance book in a science fiction book group it will likely not get much engagement? (And its irrelevance may hurt your social currency in that group).

Review Swaps
A direct swap between authors (where you review an author's book and they review yours) is a breach of Amazon's terms of service.

If however you and another random author are both promoting an Amazon giveaway at the same time and download each other's books, there is nothing to stop you from placing a review on their book.

The custom of sending out advance copies by publishers has been part of the publishing process long before the internet was born.

Unfortunately, the internet has allowed some people to game the system and in order to try to even, the playing field Amazon (and other online platforms) have tried to stop this.

Amazons terms (as I am writing this) are different for books than products but still have limitations on who can place reviews.

Book Bloggers and Review Websites
Look for the top five or ten books in your niche.

Find which blogs or review sites have reviewed those books and approach them to review your book.

This is a more focused approach than just randomly approaching book blogs for reviews. Remember that your goal is to improve your conversion rate.

If the sites that you approach have already reviewed similar books, you may assume that their target market is open to your book.

The Strategy for Contacting Reviewers
There are various strategies that you can adopt when contacting reviewers but I want to break them down into just the two options of shotgun or sniper.

- Shotgun

When you fire a shotgun it allows you to send out multiple projectiles towards your target. In this situation, you are sacrificing accuracy for the volume of projectiles and you may not get the required results. By sending out a large volume of untailored emails (perhaps using an autoresponder) from a template, you are in effect adopting a shotgun method and can be sacrificing results for volume.

- Sniper

When a sniper fires a rifle, they primarily fire one round at a time. They are sacrificing the number of rounds fired for a higher probability of hitting a single target. When you take the time to tailor each individual email you are in effect behaving more like a sniper and the extra preparation time may actually provide better results.

You may believe that as reviews are a numbers game that the more emails that you send out, the better results but before you rush out and start emailing reviewers blindly, take a deep breath and consider the following points:

- You cannot just send a review copy of a book and assume that they will read it.
- You need to give them enough information to make them read your book.
- Although we talk about building social currency and relationships (with forums and FB groups) in this situation you are promoting the book rather than yourself.
- Ensure that at least 50% of your review request focuses on the book (that information is directly from one of Amazon's top reviewers).
- Make your book stand out (you can't oversell it), tell them it's the best book in the world or include some humorous/quirky information in your email.

Ongoing reviews
Some of your seed activities will generate ongoing reviews but you cannot remain stagnant.

Adding New Content
If you update a book (and I highly suggest that you update Non Fiction where appropriate) it will help to freshen up your book and can lead to new reviews.

If you add/change a significant amount to your books (usually 10% or more) you can update this version on Amazon and this will do a few things:

- Changing the edition number on your Amazon Publishing page means that Amazon will send out the new version to all previous purchasers for free. Suddenly you have given all your readers a free gift and that can generate some reviews.
- You can update your book cover and listing description to say something like "Updated 2018 Version" etc. and freshen up your book. This can increase sales and by the nature of the numbers increase reviews.

The Amazon Terms of Service

As someone that started selling products on Amazon several years ago, I understand how frustrating some of their decisions can be. Although they are not perfect we must remember that they are in charge of their shop and we sell at their pleasure.

The guidelines may stop friends and family from reviewing your book but in the global environment that we live in, (factoring in "the six degrees of separation") it is hard not to have a connection with someone.

The guidelines state that you can't place a book review if:

- You have a personal relationship with the author of the book being reviewed, or was involved in the book's creation process (i.e. as a co-author, editor, illustrator, etc.).
- You have already placed five non-verified reviews in a week (this only restricts you from placing unverified reviews).

If Amazon decides to remove a review that means that the person cannot place another review for that book.

Disputing reviews

Unfortunately, there are people out there with ill intent and if you believe that a review has been placed unfairly you can raise a dispute with Amazon (by clicking on the report this review button). You need to say why this review breaches their guidelines.

- If the review is clearly for the wrong book/product (as I have experienced in the past) that is pretty obviously wrong.
- If the review doesn't seem genuine you can also raise a dispute.
- You can't just ask for a review to be removed because it is a one-star review, not all readers will like every book.
- Amazon can at times be slow to take action in removing reviews (if at all). Instead of spending too much time on one bad review, focus on getting more positive reviews and improving the positive to negative review ratio of your book.

Be vigilant
An important last point for this chapter!

- Not every activity that you do will be successful in getting reviews but if you don't do them you have a lot less chance.
- Always be attuned to new ways to get reviews. The Amazon World and the Amazon Terms of Service are continually evolving and if you want to evolve with them, you need to stay up to date.

Exercises
I want you and your books to succeed and as you prepare for your launch you will suddenly discover a multitude of activities that you may not have expected.

Exercise Twenty Five   Choose Ten Free Sites to Contact for Your Book Launch
Determine what you will need to supply them prior to your promotion (and have it ready):

- Do they just need your promo dates?

- Do they need a book synopsis (100,200 or 300 words)?
- Do they need a short author bio?
- Do they need a jpeg of the book cover (or will they get the info from your Amazon ASIN)?
- Do they need a specific number of days' notice to list your book promotion?

Doing this preparation now will help you immensely when your book is finally ready to launch.

Exercise Twenty Six   Choose Ten Paid Sites That You Will Contact for Your Book Launch

Bookbub.com and the likes may be above your budget but even some of the free sites have a paid option.

The paid option guarantees that they will list your promotion and can be relatively cheap.

- Look at the requirements that you prepared for the free promotions.
- Determine if you need to supply any extra information for a paid promotion.
- Ensure you have met all of their requirements.

Doing this preparation now will help you immensely when your book is finally ready to launch.

Exercise Twenty Seven   Choose a Giveaway or Countdown Deal

Although you may be some distance from your book launch, this simple exercise will make you review the information on the two options and save you time come launch time.

You can always change your mind later but at least you'll have more insight into these two options at that time. If you are close to launch then you can actually schedule your Promotion now.

Choose your preference:

- The Countdown deal.
- The Giveaway promotion $0.99.

The KDP site provides plenty of advice and instructions to carry out one of these promotions. Just pick which one you are going to do.

Chapter 11   Amazon Advertisements (Ads)

"99 percent of all statistics only tell 49 percent of the story" — **Ron DeLegge**

There has been a multitude of books and courses created on techniques and styles of marketing. One consensus that most of these resources show is that marketing is a numbers game. The Odds that your Ad will convert someone into buying a book, every time they view it are stacked largely against you. In order to calculate how effective an Ad is performing, you need to monitor it.

Online Advertising (such as Facebook Ads) can provide statistical data to allow you to analyze those numbers. After analysis, you can then determine the best options for a return on your advertising dollars.

Amazon Ads Vs Other Online Ads
Facebook (FB) Ads can be effective for creating interest in your book. Certain authors such as Mark Dawson have used FB Ads effectively in their book marketing strategies.

Although FB Ads can be cost-effective, you are competing with a lot of distractions on Facebook and subscribers may be more interested in connecting with friends rather than buying books.

Amazon book Ads are another version of an online marketing tool that allows you to analyze their effectiveness and thus optimize your Ad dollars.

Although each of the online tools can have a place in your overall marketing strategy for the purpose of this chapter we are going to focus on Amazon ads.

One of the advantages of Amazon Ads over Ads on other platforms (such as Twitter Ads or FB Ads) is that they are more focused. When you place an Amazon book Ad you are targeting a book Ad directly at a reader that is looking for books, in the place that they use to purchase their books.

There are whole books and courses written about Amazon Ads but for the purpose of this chapter, I want to give you an overview of some of the important details you need to know for your book marketing.

Sponsored Ads and Display Ads
Amazon Ads come in two main flavours, Sponsored Ads, and Display Ads.

Sponsored Ads
A Sponsored Ad is a Keyword targeted Ad that appears on the Amazon website either on the products details page or from search results.

The Ad shows based on the Keywords that you choose in your campaign. If you choose your keywords well, the Ad will be shown to readers who are likely to buy your book.

Keywords are displayed via an auction where the amount that you bid for a Keyword will determine if that Keyword displays your Ad or someone else's (when they use the keyword in an Amazon search). Although your Ad may be displayed if you have the highest bid for the Keyword, you do not get billed for the Ad unless someone clicks on it (hence the term "Pay Per Click").

Once someone clicks on your Ad they are taken to the Amazon listing page for your book.

Amazon suggests you input at least 100 Keywords for a campaign. I personally try to compile an initial spreadsheet of 100 to 300 keywords before starting a Sponsored Ad campaign.

For the purposes of Amazon Ads, the term Keyword can refer to a whole sentence and not just one word. When setting up a campaign you could class the word "Fiction" as a keyword but also the sentence "Science Fiction Dystopian Future".

You can include book titles and other authors in your genre but be careful that you don't annoy their readers.

A tool such as KDP Rocket can save you hours of research.

After a few weeks, you should review which words are getting impressions and which words are converting to sales.

Display Ads
A Display Ad is displayed based on a set of targeted criteria such as interests, gender, age group etc.

Display Ads can display on the product details page or as Ads on the front of a Kindle (where the Kindle owner has allowed Ads and they meet the criteria).

This targeted Ad can have the front cover of your book actually filling the whole screen of a Kindle.

Limitations of the Ads
If we equate the potential buyers that interact with our book marketing as a train full of passengers on a journey. The Ad is the station where the prospective buyers start off and the destination we want them to reach is purchasing our book at the Amazon checkout.

Unfortunately, there are lots of other stops on the route and not all of the passengers will stay on the train until the end of the line.

- When the Ad is displayed through Amazon (either as a thumbnail with other books in Amazon's storefront or on the front of someone's kindle) a large percentage of the people will consciously or subconsciously blank out the Ad. You've lost your first passengers.
- Out of the people that actually acknowledge the book Ad (by looking at it for more than a split second) only a small percentage will click on the Ad. More Passengers gone.
- Out of the people that click on the Ad (to find out more information) only a small percentage of them will actually be engaged by the description or the other information provided. We are running out of passengers fast.
- Even when you get a customer all the way to the Amazon Checkout, they may get buyer's remorse and decide not to purchase a copy of the book.
- You may have just lost your Last passenger on this train but the more Ads you run, the more potential trains and passengers you are attracting.

As this is a numbers game, you want more trains and more people staying on those trains until they reach the destination (Amazon's checkout).

Your Ad Dashboard

Once you have submitted a few Ad campaigns your Dashboard for your Ad Campaigns can look pretty crowded. Especially if you have had ads rejected along the way.

For ease of viewing, you only want to see your live (running) Ads in your dashboard.

In order to only view the Ads that are running if you click on the word "Status", it will automatically organize the ads in order or submission. This will mean that your Current Ads are not visible at the top of the table. Clicking on the word "status" again will reorder them so that your latest running Ads are now displayed at the top of your dashboard.

Monitoring Your Ads and Identifying Outliers

The KDP Platform allows you to run various reports on your Amazon Ads but when you are first starting out you may want to monitor your campaigns every day.

ACOS

Advertising Cost of Sales (ACOS) is one of the main metrics to monitor when checking your campaign's performance. The ACOS is the amount spent on advertising to achieve an actual sale as a percentage of the sales price. If the sale price of your product is $10.00 and your ACOS is 10% then the cost of your advertising to achieve this sale is approximately $1.00.

In KDP the ACOS is automatically calculated and displayed in your campaign.

If you have an Ad campaign that is running quite successfully and suddenly everything grinds to a halt, don't panic. No matter how much preparation and analysis you undertake, there will be outliers/occurrences along the way that seem to throw a spanner in the works.

I personally had a successful campaign that had been running for months. I was getting a similar number of daily clicks on the Ad and the conversion rate was equating to around the same ACOS.

I tend to check my sales data at the same time each day, so when I checked the campaign one day and found no sales but the number of clicks had remained constant I was only slightly concerned. On day two, when I was still getting clicks on my Ad but no Sales, I was starting to wonder what was happening.

By day three I was getting a bit anxious. None of my books were selling and I had checked that they were all available for sale.

A couple of days later my sales reverted to their normal levels and the ACOS recovered, but what had gone wrong?

It was the weekend of Black Friday and Cyber Monday and that had been the issue. I suddenly remembered back to my product selling days on Amazon. Although we expect Sales of products to increase as we head into the fourth quarter and holiday sales, this usually occurs after Black Friday weekend. During that weekend most shoppers expect huge discounts on products (These are sometimes referred to as Tire Kickers). If your product is at the normal price, a shopper may click on your Ad in a shopping frenzy but this will rarely convert to book Sales.

Unlike traditional products, KDP doesn't allow you to post your book under sales prices (notwithstanding Countdown deals) so you may want to pause your book ads over this weekend.

Review Impacts
Although monitoring and adjusting keywords can help to optimize your conversion rate you need to take into account any changes to your book content or listings.

Initially, your book cover and title will stay the same so the two main variables could be your book description or the number of reviews that you accrue.

Ideally, you should minimize the variables to make it easier to analyze your results.

Stick with the same description on your listing for the first sixty days and log the number of reviews that you have in relation to your conversion rate.

Historical Ad Campaign details

I'll use one of my old Ad campaigns to put this in real terms:

- This was a targeted Display Ad campaign that was aimed at specific people, with specific interests.
- Out of 27,000 impressions for one book (that was selling reasonably well) I received 160 clicks (approx. 0.6%).
- I had a paperback version of this non-fiction book (so most of the time the Amazon Sales dashboard didn't show the click to sales conversions) and the conversion rate was almost 50%. So 160 clicks gave me around 80 sales.
- So out of 27,000 impressions, I received a sales ratio of approximately 0.3%
- By running various campaigns and optimizing listings etc you can improve your results but if you look at the figures above and see a conversion rate of 0.3% you realize that the nature of the game is to get the best product in front of as many of the right people in the best way.

Return on your Advertising Investment

Know Your Profit Margins

When you look at your ACOS, it is important that you realize that the sales revenue and your potential profits (or book royalties) are not the same things.

The Sales Revenue is what Amazon receives for your book and the royalties (your profits) are what Amazon actually pays you from the book sales.

I know that some people glaze over with numbers but as it's important that you understand the financials of your marketing so I'll break things down for you.

For simplicity let's assume that you are running an Ad campaign, and for each $8 you spend on your ad you achieve $10 in book sales. We will also assume that Amazon is paying you 70% of the books sales revenue as royalties.

- That gives you an ACOS of $8 (expenditure) ÷ $10 (the Value of the sales) x 100 (to create a percentage) = 80%.
- If you looked at only those figures, at an 80% cost ratio it would seem that you are making 20% profit on your Ads.
- In reality, If you only receive $7 (70% of the books sales revenue) that changes your ratio to $8 (expenditure) ÷ $7 (the amount Amazon pays you) x 100 (to create a percentage) = 114%.

This means that you are actually spending 14% more on Ads than you are making from your book sales.

What ACOS Do You Need
Knowing that an ACOS percentage of less than 100% doesn't mean that we are actually making money tells us that we need a better idea of what a good ACOS is.

The main place to start is the true break-even point for your ACOS.

Assuming that your Royalty rate for your Target Ad market is 70% then your ACOS break-even point should be 70%.

- Given an ACOS of $7 (expenditure) ÷ $10 (the Value of the sales) x 100 (to create a percentage) = 70%.
- In reality, If you only receive $7 (70% of the books Sales revenue) that changes your ratio to one of $7 (expenditure) ÷ $7 (the amount Amazon pays you) x 100 (to create a percentage) = 100%.
- If you are spending 100% of our profits on Ad campaigns you are just at break even.

I understand that there may be tax retentions from Amazon and other costs not factored into these royalty payments. The main point to understand is that if your ACOS is over 70% you are below break-even.

Your own business plan and Cashflow will mean that only you can determine what return you want from your book Ads. Whatever your target ACOS, you definitely need to know when an Ad is costing you money.

Choose the Correct Keyword Bid Price
When you start an Amazon-sponsored book Ad based on Keyword searches, you are in effect entering into an auction scenario.

CPC
The price that you bid for your keyword is known as the Cost Per Click (CPC) and can determine if your Ad is actually displayed, or not.

If three authors are running an Ad using the Keyword "Thriller":

- Author A bids $0.10 a click for this Keyword.
- Author B bids $0.20 a click for this Keyword.
- Author C bids $0.80 a click for this Keyword.
- Author C wins the bid and their Ad can be displayed on Amazons sales page, whenever someone types in the word Thriller in an Amazon search.

The model for these Keyword Ads is referred to as Pay Per Click (PPC), this means that you as the advertiser only pay when someone clicks on your Ad.

It might seem great that author C has an Ad that people will see, but the fact that they will be charged $0.80 for every click on that Ad may mean it's not profitable.

Conversion Rates

For Amazon book Ads when we refer to the conversion rate, we mean the number of buyer clicks that convert into actual book sales.

e.g. if only one person buys a book from every ten people who click on your book Ad, the conversion rate is 10%.

As you pay for each click, it is important to set your bid price correctly.

- Author A bids $0.10 at 10% conversion rate they need 10 clicks for a sale, so a sale costs them (10 x $0.10) $1.00.
- Author B bids $0.20 at 10% conversion rate they need 10 clicks for a sale, so a sale costs them (10 x $0.20) $2.00.
- Author C bids $0.80 conversion rate they need 10 clicks for a sale, so a sale costs them (10 x $0.80) $8.00.

If we assume they are receiving royalties (as in the above section on profit margins) of $7 a sale.

Author C is winning the Bid and displaying their Ad but it is not profitable as it costs $8 for every $7 of royalties (or profits).

Although the bid price is important, you should also look at ways to optimize your conversion rates.

Ensuring that you have a great book cover, title, content and a great book listing will help increase conversion rates.

Don't Accept the Default Bid

When you start an Amazon Ad campaign based on keywords, Amazon has an initial setting for a default bid for the words ($0.25), you do not need to accept this bid.

- This isn't the type of auction where you just have to place a huge bid to win. Amazon tends to suggest default bids for keywords that are higher than they need to be.

- Amazon will also offer suggested bids for a word. If the suggested bid seems extortionate, look for alternative words.
- Start with a lower bid of around $0.10 a click and increase it as required.
- If you add words during a live Ad campaign, be aware that the default bid will still be set, whatever your current bid for your other keywords.
- Set your bid before you input your keywords, as you can't change from $0.25 or you have to delete the keywords and input again at your lower bid rate.
- I personally tend to set my initial bid to $0.15.

Have a Set Budget and Be Patient
The minimum budget that the Amazon KDP system allows per Ad campaign is $100.

If $100 seems a bit expensive, it should be noted that you don't have to spend the full amount of this budget.

If your available Advertising budget is less than $100, set the Ad budget to the minimum $100 but ensure that you know what your real budget is. Pause your Ad when it reaches your true amount.

Ways to ensure that your Ad expenditure doesn't reach $100:

- Set the Campaign over a longer period (e.g. three months).
- Set the CPC at a lower level.
- Set the Pacing of the Campaign to "Spread campaign evenly over its duration.
- Set a daily campaign budget.

During the first week of your Ad campaign, the ACOS may look terrible, you need to monitor it but also give it time to gain some traction.

Review your campaign weekly and look for improvements. Don't panic and stop a campaign just because week one results are bad.

Factor your Book's lLst Price into your Advertising strategy
The price of your book is one element that you need to take into account when setting your advertising budget.

A Kindle book that is listed on Amazon for $0.99 will recoup fewer royalties (for the sale of one book) than another book listed at $9.00.

It would be nice If it was as simple as pricing your books higher to make your money on your Ads.

Unfortunately, there are many factors that determine the price of your book, as we discussed in the chapter on pricing.

You may be advertising the first book in a series that is permanently free. This will not provide a relevant ACOS on that book but may have a knock on effect to the sales revenue from other books in the series.

You may have your books priced at various price points to appeal to readers with different budgets.

As you can't always rely on the price of your book to determine the return on your advertising budget, invest your Ad dollars wisely.

Potential Credit Card Fees
In order to analyze the best allocation of your advertising budget, although you may initially just run one campaign, most successful authors will build that up to running several campaigns at once.

A cautionary note to overseas authors.

A large percentage of indie authors (worldwide) sell on Amazon and not all of them have bank accounts in The US or the UK.

If you are a using a Non-US / Non-UK credit card for your Ad campaigns, you may incur exchange fees on your monthly transactions.

This means that if you have several Ad campaigns running and your monthly clicks cost only a few cents you may end up paying several dollars extra for those clicks (due to credit card fees).

When you are first starting out, these fees can add up. Once you start to run multiple campaigns, carefully monitor which Ad campaigns work and cut the non-profitable campaigns.

Exercises

By the time your Book Launch arrives, you will have lots to do and it may seem as there aren't enough hours in the day.

Although I have included a few calculations in this chapter, the purpose was primarily to introduce you to the concepts for Amazon Ads. I have kept any calculations in the exercises below as reasonably simple.

You want to have your first book Ad campaign ready to go within the first thirty days of your book going live. One of the best pieces of advice I can give you is to start preparing for the campaign in advance.

Exercise Twenty Eight   Compile a Keyword List for Your Sponsored Ad

For your first sponsored Ad you should start with 100-300 Keywords,

The easiest way to compile your list is to use software such as KDP Rocket but if you are on a limited budget you might want to use the manual option.

Unlike the seven keywords in your book listing, you can use other author's names in your Ad keywords.

Some keyword suggestions:

- The names of authors with similar books.

- The names of books in the same genres.
- The types of sentences people would type in when looking for books in your genre.

Ensure that you choose close matches as if your keywords are aimed at the wrong readers it can disappoint and annoy them.

Exercise Twenty Nine   Set Your Advertising Budget
From the chapter on commitment you will be aware of your available capital.

From the money that you have available, determine how much you will commit to your marketing budget.

- This doesn't have to be a huge amount but you have to start somewhere.
- Ideally budget for an ongoing monthly amount.
- Commit to an initial minimum amount and ensure that you keep to it.

As you work through a campaign your budget may change but this exercise will give you a starting point.

Exercise Thirty   Calculate the Royalties for Your Book
From the pricing chapter, you should now have determined the initial price for your book.

I realize that you may have to deduct taxes and other considerations from your royalties but I just want you to set a baseline here.

Sometimes authors are surprised at the small amount of royalties that they receive for their book. For the purpose of this exercise, you are going to calculate the amount of hard cash you will get for the sale of your book.

A. Assume that you are receiving 70% Royalties.
- Multiply the price of your book by 70 and divide it by 100 to get your 70% royalties.

B. Assume that you are receiving 30% Royalties.

- Multiply the price of your book by 30 and divide it by 100 to get your 70% royalties.

I know that this is a simple exercise but lots of authors focus on the writing and sometimes forget about the money.

It can be quite sobering when you look at these numbers.

Chapter 12   Other Formats

"Obsession with broad diversification is the sure road to mediocrity"
– John Neff

Although this book is primarily about digital publishing through KDP, a lot of the information in this book (such as book titles, book covers, book listings etc.) is relevant to other formats of your book.

This chapter is not meant as an all-encompassing reference for all other formats of your book.

It is just here to provide a reminder of the potential to sell other formats of your books and the natural progression of Indie Authors. You can start selling Kindle books but you also have the opportunity for wider distribution of your content.

From my personal experience of selling physical products through Amazon I have always looked at Amazon as a stepping stone. If you only sell your products on Amazon you are giving them a lot of control.

I have always suggested to new product sellers that they build their own e-commerce site and transition to having between 50-70% of their sales volume away from Amazon.

When it comes to books, you may not want to setup your own online book shop. Luckily if you don't want your own bookshop, there are lots of platforms out there to enable you wider distribution of your books.

Why You Would Want to Sell Outside of Amazon

It's worth noting that Amazon is currently estimated to be responsible for approximately 65% of all online books sales (and that will continue to grow) in both print and digital formats.

Choosing wider distribution doesn't mean that you are just being greedy.

As an independent author / publisher, if you are only publishing on Kindle KDP you are giving up a lot of your independence. If Amazon suddenly changes their policies it can have a big impact on Authors relying solely on them for book royalties:

- If they decide to change the percentage of royalties that they pay, you could suddenly see a large drop in this income stream.
- If they decide to limit access to new authors (or charge to list on their platform) it could make it harder for authors to publish their books.

It's Amazon's playing field and if you limit yourself to them as a distributor, you must play by their rules.

Procrastination

When you publish your first book you may choose to publish it in multiple formats at the same time.

If you have never published before you may underestimate how much time it takes to edit your book in different formats (or the extra marketing) required for the different publishing platforms.

I'd suggest publishing your book initially on Kindle (and maybe through Createspace) in order to learn the ropes.

You will no doubt make some mistakes and even with the information in this book, you learn best through your own experiences.

If you try wider distribution at the start you may be overwhelmed and this can lead to procrastination.

Publishing your first book is a bit like ripping off a band aid. It gets easier after the first one but it can still be a little painful.

Other eBook distribution

Formatting your manuscript for KDP will allow it to be distributed as an eBook for kindles but further editing the same manuscript can enable its wider distribution.

The extra time (and potential cost) of this editing shouldn't be seen as a barrier, as for some formats the extra editing is relatively minor.

If you begin your publishing under the KDP Select programme, you are tied in to a 90 day exclusive agreement. If you choose not to include your book in KDPS (or decide not to continue in KDPS after your initial 90 days), there are various ways to distribute your book as an eBook

Independent Distribution

Opening your own account with the likes of KOBO or Apple (iBooks) will allow you to distribute your eBook through their platform. As with KDP you need to ensure that your book is formatted to meet the requirements of each platform.

Each platform takes a commission (percentage) on the sales price of each copy of your eBook that they sell.

The fact that we are indie authors can sometimes mean that we yearn to control the whole publishing process. Having a broad understanding of the main steps of the process should be our goal but if we tie up all of our time learning new skills (and the various types of formatting), we might not have time to write.

Bulk distribution

As an Indie Author time is one of our most precious resources and using a distribution service such as Smashwords.com or Draft2digital.com can allow us a one stop shop to reach multiple sellers.

The basic functions of these two sites are that you upload one document and they handle the distribution to multiple sales platforms such as Apple or Kobo.

Each of these distribution services retains a commission on the sales price on top of the commission retained by the sales platform.

Here's an example of selling a copy of your book on Kobo through Draft2Digital:

A. If your book is priced at $2.00.
- Kobo would retain their commission of $1.10 (55%).
- Draft2digital would retain their commission of $0.20 (10%).
- You would receive $0.70.
B. If your book is priced at $10.00.
- Kobo would retain their commission of $3.00 (30%).
- Draft2digital would retain their commission of $1.00 (10%).
- You would receive $7.00.

As you can see here, the commission percentages may change on the sales platform (based on the list price) but Draft2Digitals commission percentage stays the same.

It might seem like you are giving up a lot of your hard earned commission by using a distribution service but it saves you the time and trouble of registering and setting up multiple accounts yourself.

Physical (Print) Book Formats

Once you have done the hard work of creating your manuscript adding a physical version of your manuscript for sale should be seen as a natural progression. With today's Print on Demand Publishing (POD) opportunities, your initial costs are primarily editing.

You can even list the physical version of your book on Amazon and link the listings so that any marketing for your eBook contributes to your physical book sales.

I appreciate that selling print versions of your books through Amazon, can be seen as putting all your eggs in one basket, but I am only suggesting this as a first step for your books.

Createspace
Createspace.com is a free publishing service that allows you to publish your books and sell them via Print on Demand. Originally two companies CustomFlix and Booksurge where acquired by Amazon in 2005 and merged to become Createspace by 2009.

At the time of writing this Createspace is one of the main publishers that allows you to print physical copies of your books on demand. The listing of your physical book can be linked to your digital listing so that customers have the option of purchasing either format when they click on your book on Amazon. When you upload a formatted manuscript on Createspace it will ask you if you want to create a Kindle Version of your book at the same time.

The Kindle publisher, KDP also allows you to create a print version of your book at the same time that you upload your manuscript for kindle.

With Amazon publishing, you have tw options:

- Produce both your digital book and your print book through KDP.
- Produce your digital book through one of the two platforms and the print version through the other.

Just as Amazon no longer provides Createspace services but has focused solely on KDP Print. It pays to be familiar with this platform but keep yourself up to date for further changes in the market.

Formatting Differences between Digital and Print.
In a digital book you want hyperlinks in the Table of Contents (TOC) pages to enhance navigation and benefit the reader. You may add other hyperlinks throughout the book to online resources.

In a print book hyperlinks are not only unnecessary but can cause formatting issues in the way that the text displays:

- The blue header font may look good on a kindle fire but when it is printed in black and white through Createspace, it may come out grey or hard to read in the print version.
- If you don't take the hyperlinks out of a TOC, your book may look fine on the digital proof reader (as it is designed to view digital books) but this formatting can look bad on the "Look inside" feature for the paperback on amazon. I realized on one of my books that the TOC hadn't been updated, which meant that in the print version, the number "4" had replaced all of the page numbers in the TOC.
- When I updated the TOC in Word, everything looked fine. I went through the approval process again and even though the digital proof reader looked ok, once the listing was updated on Amazon it was ugly. I used the look inside feature and the text lines in the TOC all had lines struck through or where greyed out. Not a first impression I wanted readers to have of one of my books.

Linking the Various Formats
Ensure that the book titles are exactly the same on all listings:

- If you accidentally mistype a listing title (even something simple as omitting a comma), it will not be linked to the other formats.

- If your listings aren't automatically linked, contact Createspace and they will usually sort this in 3-5 business days. They can take action quicker than the estimated timetable but I always assume the worst case scenario for planning purposes.

Digital Book Formats

When people think of digital books they tend to visualize the written word but audio versions of your book are also classed as digital formats.

It is estimated that in the next couple of years, audio book sales will rise to that of eBook sales so why not get ready now?

I know a lot of new authors feel that if they are going to turn their book into an audio book, only there voice will do.

They tend to underestimate the time effort and technology required to produce an audio file of sufficient quality.

I understand that in our technological age, people can do amazing things, such as making a full length movie on an IPhone. I would argue that is only because these have developed skills in this field and you might not have.

Through companies sites as Findawayvoices.com you can find narrators that suit you and your budget.

Audible.com

Audible.com is a subsidiary of Amazon and is their way of selling audiobooks.

Just like KDP is a way to distribute your eBooks, Audible is the way to distribute your audiobooks.

They also have similarities in that they have subscription services or separate retail options.

ACX

What is Audiobook Creation Exchange (ACX)?

The ACX website defines it as: *"a marketplace where authors, literary agents, publishers, and other Rights Holders can connect with narrators, engineers, recording studios, and other Producers capable of producing a finished audiobook. The result: More audiobooks will be made".*

For a long time ACX was the only way to sell your audiobooks through Audible.

Although KDP allows you to upload a document from most word processors to transform them to a Kindle format, ACX requires that your audiobook meets stricter criteria:

- It must be consistent in overall sound formatting.
- It must be comprised of all mono or all stereo files.
- It must include opening and closing credits.
- It must include a retail sample that is between one and five minutes long.
- It must be recorded by a human.

The full criteria is available on their website but we need to remember that the reasons for these criteria is to ensure that the audio quality is maintained for the listeners.

Contracts

In years gone by traditional publishers tied in authors publishing rights for lengthy periods.

ACX has also historically locked in the rights of authors for extremely lengthy periods.

Seven years was not unheard of for ACX to lock in your distribution rights for exclusive distribution through ACX. Ensure that you know how long you are committing to before signing away your rights.

Exercises

Once you have your digital book live, it is not much extra work to publish a print version of the same book. You may decide to publish them both at the same time but whatever your timeframe is I would suggest you schedule in production of other formats before your run out of steam.

Exercise Thirty One   Schedule the Production of Your Print Book

Don't let the fact that your print book isn't ready stop you launching your first kindle book.

Ensure that you have a timetable and take into account:

- The extra time, cost and skill for editing.
- The need for a full book cover (not just a jpeg for your eBook front).
- The text for the back of your book (this is another chance to market your book).

Even if you are only planning to launch your print book a few weeks after your digital book, remain flexible.

THE KEY ELEMENTS FOR (INDIE) AUTHOR SUCCESS

Annex A   Summary and Resources

Summary
On our journey (together) through this book, we have looked at the elements that you need to successfully publish on Kindle.

Although we have delved into some of these elements in depth, I encourage all my fellow Indie Authors to build their education in publishing.

There are some great resources out there for indie authors and I personally love searching out new tools and checking them out. To save you some time I have included a list of some of my favourite resources here in this annex. I challenge you to sample some of these resources yourself and find ones that resonate with you.

Reviews
I hope that you have enjoyed our journey through this book as much as I enjoyed writing it. Having read the chapter on Reviews you will now know how important they are to the success of your books. I love to hear where my writing has helped others and I would be so happy and grateful if you would please take 5 minutes to share your experience, by leaving a review for this book on Amazon.

When you publish your own book, don't be afraid to ask for reviews. Remember the quote at the start of the book?

*"Marketing your book is sharing what you love, with people who look forward to hearing about it." – **Joanna Penn***

Free Stuff

Free Downloads

If you have purchased a digital version of this book (or even if you bought a print version), you may like individual checklists and templates to write on.

The following documents are available to download (as PDFs) from my website gedcusack.com.

- Annex E – Book Launch Checklist – KDP Book Free Downloads
- Annex F – Book Review Options checklist – KDP Book Free Downloads
- Annex G – Book cover Brief – KDP Book Free Downloads

Free Online Course

For anyone interested in building an online business, I've created a free online course (to help you determine the right online business for you).

Follow this link for access to this free course http://creating-clarity-from-chaos.thinkific.com/courses/take/3-steps-to-choosing-your-profitable-online-business/

Recommended Resources

Books

- Better sleep For The Overachiever – Anne Bartolucci
- Mastering Amazon Ads: an Authors guide – Brian D. Meeks
- 5,000 Words Per Hour – Chris Fox
- Write to Market – Chris Fox
- Strangers to Superfans – David Gaughran
- 527 Quotes for Entrepreneurs – Ged Cusack

- How to Choose a Writing Coach: A Beginner's guide – Ged Cusack
- Naked Review: How to get book Reviews – Gisela Hausmann
- The Healthy Writer – Joanna Penn & Euan Lawson
- How To Make a Living with Your Writing – Joanna Penn
- How to Market a book – Joanna Penn
- Successful Self-Publishing – Joanna Penn
- The Successful Author Mindset – Joanna Penn
- How I sold 30,000 eBooks on Amazon's Kindle – Martin Crosbie
- The Writer's Guide to Training Your Dragon – Scott Baker
- Quick Cheats for Writing With Dragon – Scott Baker

Book Promotion sites
- Readingdeals.com: http://readingdeals.com/confirm-ebook/free/id=54538
- readers in the know .com: http://www.readersintheknow.com/home
- readfree.ly: http://www.readfree.ly/
- prettyhot.com: http://pretty-hot.com/submit-your-book/
- newfreekindlebooks.com: http://newfreekindlebooks.com/authors/
- ebooklister.net: http://www.ebooklister.net/submit.php
- armadilloebooks.com: http://www.armadilloebooks.com/submit-free-ebooks/
- bookangel.co.uk: http://bookangel.co.uk/submit-a-book/
- bookbongo.com: http://bookbongo.com/submit/
- bookoftheday.org: http://bookoftheday.org/add-book/
- bookbub.com: https://www.bookbub.com/home/
- Ask David: https://askdavid.com/book-promotion/

Podcasts
- The Creative Penn – thecreativepenn.com: hosted by Joanna Penn.
- Mark Dawson's Self-Publishing formula – Selfpublishingformula.com: hosted by James Blatch & Mark Dawson.
- Book Marketing Show – Kindlepreneur.com: hosted by Dave Chesson.
- The Sell More Books show – Sellmorebooksshow.com: hosted by Jim Kukral & Bryan Cohen.
- Ben Settle – bensettle.com: hosted by Ben Settle.

Twitter book promotion accounts
- @kindlenews
- @DigitalBkToday
- @kindleebooks
- @Kindlestuff
- @KindleEbooksUK
- @KindleBookKing
- @KindleFreeBook
- @Freebookdude
- @Kindlefinds
- @Kindlebookreview
- @free
- @free_kindle
- @KindleFreeBook
- @4FreeKindleBook
- @FreeKindleStuff
- @KindleUpdates
- @kindleebooks
- @Kindlestuff
- @kindlesfnovel

- @kindlemysbook
- @Kindle_Freebies
- @hashltrd
- @100freebooks
- @kindletop100
- @kindleowners
- @hashltrd
- @100freebooks
- @kindletop100
- @kindleowners
- @IndAuthorSucess
- @FreeEbooksDaily
- @AwesometasticBk
- @Bookyrnextread
- @Kindle_promo
- @CheapKindleDly
- @KindleDaily
- @BookBub

Websites to host additional Author bios etc.
- Ask David – http://askdavid.com/book-promotion
- readers in the know .com –
  http://www.readersintheknow.com/home
- authorsden.com –
  https://www.authorsden.com/join/Default.asp
- authormarketingclub.com –
  http://authormarketingclub.com/members/submit-your-book/

Useful online tools
- Automatic HTML Description Tool:
  https://kindlepreneur.com/amazon-book-description-generator/

- Automatic Universal Review Link Creation Tool :https://www.rpbook.co.uk/tools/toolpage.php?tool=amazon-review-link
- Universal Amazon affiliate Link tool: https://kindlepreneur.com/genius-amazon-associate-link-tool/
- Universal ASIN Link: https://www.booklinker.net/

Other Useful Sites
- Chandler Bolts Self-Publishing school – https://self-publishingschool.com/
- Chris Fox – http://www.chrisfoxwrites.com/
- Dave Chesson's Kindlepreneur – https://kindlepreneur.com/
- Derek Murphy – https://www.creativindie.com/
- Ged Cusack – https://Gedcusack.com/
- Joanna Penn – https://www.thecreativepenn.com/
- Jonathan Green – https://servenomaster.com/
- Pat Flynn's Smart Passive income (SPI) – https://courses.smartpassiveincome.com/

Annex B   Glossary

I understand that a lot of the terms here are common tongue to most but as this book is aimed at a broad spectrum of readers I have tried to be as inclusive as possible.

At the time of writing this book, the information provided below is current but I accept no responsibility for changes to external sites and sources at a later date.

A

ADVERTISEMENTS (ADS)   A notice or announcement that promotes an event or product. With Book Ads, this is normally a short punchy text accompanied by an image of the book cover.

ADVERTISING COST OF SALES (ACOS)   A   calculation that takes into account the amount spent on advertising to achieve an actual sale as a percentage of the sales price. Online sales platforms such as Amazon calculate the ACOS automatically and it can be displayed in reports. If the sale price of your product is $10.00 and your ACOS is 10% then the cost of your advertising to achieve this sale is approximately $1.00.

ALGORITHM   A set of steps in mathematics (and computer science) that are performed to provide the results of a calculation or automated reasoning task. The steps are performed in a set process and in relation to computers are followed automatically.

AMAZON (AN ABBREVIATION OF AMAZON.COM)   The largest online retailer in the United States and the parent company of various other Amazon online retailers, such as Amazon.co.uk in the UK.

AMAZONS SEARCH ALGORITHM   The calculation that Amazon uses from various factors (on its platform) to determine the popularity of a product, and various other details about its products listing.

ASIN (AMAZON STANDARD IDENTIFICATION NUMBER)   A ten character alphanumeric indicator that Amazon uses to identify individual items in its catalogue.

B

BATCHING   The activity of arranging activities into sets or groups of similar activities. When it comes to publishing, two activities such as writing and editing can require different mindsets. Allocating separate writing and editing time is a way of batching activities to be more efficient.

BERNIE CONVENTION   An international agreement governing copyright established in Berne Switzerland (in1886). This introduced the concept that copyright exists the moment a work is "fixed". The term Fixed in this context refers to the idea of being fixed in a tangible form (e.g. the words of a song being written down).

BEST SELLER RANKING (BSR)   Amazon allocates every product in its digital catalogue a number that indicates its position (or ranking). This number can decrease if the product becomes more popular or increase if it becomes less popular.

BIO (BIOGRAPHY)   A detailed description of someone's life. Online biographies tend to be more abridged than actual books written as biographies and tend to focus on specific activities that the person has done in relation to an article, course or product.

BLOG (abbreviated from weblog)   A regularly updated website or web page written in a more informal, conversational style than more traditional websites.

BLOGGER   A person or persons who updates a blog (frequently).

BOOKMARKS BAR   The Bookmarks bar is a toolbar across the top of your computer screen when you are logged on to the internet through a web browser (such as Google Chrome). The bookmarks are links to other websites and allow you to navigate more quickly to websites that you frequently visit.

BRAND   A brand is a type of product manufactured by a particular company under a particular name (e.g. Coca-cola).

BROWSER   Also known as a Web Browser (although some may think that Google is the only Browser), it is a digital platform that allows internet users to navigate their way through the trillions of bits of information on the net.

C

CASHFLOW   The financial capital flowing in and out of your accounts (positive Cashflow means you have more coming in than going out).

CATEGORY   The Specific area of The Amazon Site that a product is listed in (e.g. a Tire may be listed in the Automotive Category).

CATEGORY STRINGS A list of categories and subcategories that drill down from a broad subject category (On Amazon) to a specific subcategory. An example of a Category string is – Kindle Store > Kindle eBooks > Comics & Graphic Novels > Teen & Young Adult.

CODE An abbreviation for the terms computer code or Computer languages.

CODING The art of creating computer programs, apps or other digital creations using computer languages.

COPY AND PASTE A well know term for the functions in word processing software such as MS Word, you highlight the text in one document (or application) and copy that text into another document (or application). This is the modern version of scrapbooking where a pair of scissors and a glue stick have been replaced with a computer mouse.

COPYRIGHT Copyright legally protects your original works like artwork, books, computer programs, drawings, films, music, and sound recordings. You may use the symbol © to help you demonstrate that you claim copyright in a particular work. Your protection is free and applies automatically from the creation of the work (in most cases it applies for your lifetime plus 50 - 100 years) in countries where the Berne Convention Applies.

D

DICTATION Recording words that will be typed or transcribed at a later date. In the past Tape recorders and mp3 recorders have been used for dictation but smartphones are now the tool of choice for lots of people's dictation.

DIGITAL RIGHTS MANAGEMENT (DRM) A system designed to provide copyright protection for digital media by restricting the way consumers can copy the content they've purchased.

E

EMPLOYER IDENTIFICATION NUMBER (EIN) A unique nine-digit number allocated by the IRS (of The USA) to businesses for the purpose of identification.

F

FACEBOOK (AN ABBREVIATION FOR FACEBOOK.COM) A social networking website that makes it easy for you to connect and share with your family and friends online.

FIVERR (AN ABBREVIATION FOR FIVERR.COM) An online platform where you can hire freelancers to carry out almost any activity that can be performed by a computer. The title comes from the fact that you can hire people for tasks starting as low as five US Dollars.

G

GENRE A genre is a specific type of book, film etc that identifies the type of content. Romance is a common genre but can be broken down into sub-genres such as romantic comedy.

GOOGLE DOCS Google docs is a word processor that is part of the free online software office suite, supplied by the Google Company (within its Google Drive service).

GOOGLE CHROME Is one of the most used Web browsers, supplied by the Goole Company.

GOOGLE CHROME EXTENSION A piece of software that can be added to the google chrome platform (an extension) that allows you to get extra functions out of Google Chrome.

H

HTML (HYPER TEXT MARKUP LANGUAGE) A standardized system used to format text when building websites or creating content on the world wide web.

HYPERLINK A digital link within a document that takes you directly to another location. The new location can be within the same document of the book or elsewhere such as a website.

I

INDEPENDENT (INDIE) AUTHOR An independent author refers to an author that is the creative director of their own books from concept to completion and beyond. An indie author means that there is no separate publisher involved.

INFLUENCERS A person or company that has an established following and can influence their followers' opinions or buying habits.

INSTAGRAM (AN ABBREVIATION OF INSTAGRAM.COM)

An online mobile photo-sharing, video-sharing, and social networking service that enables its users to take pictures and videos, and share them either publicly or privately on the app, as well as through a variety of other social networking platforms, such as Facebook, Twitter, Tumblr, and Flickr.

INTELLECTUAL PROPERTY (IP)

Intellectual Property a term that refers to intangible property created as a result of creativity. In legal terms, your ownership rights to your IP are governed by similar laws to those governing copyrights. Licensing of publishing rights for various territories can take various forms so any author should seek professional advice before signing away these rights.

INTERNATIONAL STANDARD BOOK NUMBER (ISBN)

An ISBN is an international ten digit number that is unique to a book (whether in print or digital format) and identifies specific details about that book. Different formats of the same book will require a separate ISBN.

J

JUNGLE SCOUT

This is a paid Google Chrome extension sold by a company through their website Junglescout.com. It allows you to analyze product listing information (when searching on amazon.com through the Google Chrome browser.

K

KINDLE DIRECT PUBLISHING (KDP)   A service supplied by the Amazon company that allows you to upload and publish a book to sell on the Amazon platform.

KDP ROCKET   A piece of research software sold by Dave Chesson that analyses data and helps you determine the optimum keywords and categories for your book listing.

KDP SPY   A piece of research software that analyses data and helps you determine the optimum keywords and categories for your book listing.

KEYWORD   In relation to a search on Amazon.com the keyword is a word or term that the algorithm identifies as relevant to a specific book or product on the platform.

K-LYTICS   A piece of research software that analyses data and helps you determine the optimum genres for profitable publishing.

L

LISTING (AN ABBREVIATION OF AMAZON SELLER LISTING)
In order for customers to find products on Amazon the items need to be listed in Amazon's digital catalogue. The listing includes all of the information about a product that the seller has input, including images, descriptions, and pricing.

M

MICROSOFT (MS) WORD   A word processing software product sold by the Microsoft Company.

MONEY POOR A term that means what it says, you do not have enough money available to meet your requirements.

N

NEURALLY Relating to, or affecting a nerve or the nervous system.

O

OPPORTUNITY COSTS This relates to the potential costs (in time or money) that you are incurring by investing in a specific endeavor. If you invested $100 in a lottery ticket and didn't win the cost would be your $100 stake plus any potential revenue that you could have made from investing that money elsewhere.

OUTSIDE OF THE BOX The term outside of the box usually precedes the word "thinking" and refers to the method of approaching problems in new and innovative ways. The premise being that standard thinking is between the lines if a box.

P

PAY PER CLICK (PPC) An auction type system for an internal advertising platform on Amazon.com. Customers input words in their searches for products and if you have a winning bid in that words auction your Ads show up. You pay the amount that you have bid if the customer then clicks on your product Ad.

PERMA-FREE A shortened version of the term permanently free. Rather than having an item (such as a book) on sale only for a specific period, this item is permanently free. It has become popular in recent times to have the first book in a series listed as permanently free online. The theory is that once a reader tries your first book, they will hopefully want to purchase the rest of the books in that series.

PINTEREST (PINTEREST.COM) *A social network that allows users to visually share, and discover new interests by posting images or videos to their own or others' boards.*

PRICE POINT A term for the suggested retail price of a product. This is set to allow the product to compete with similar products in the marketplace. Although the price takes into account the price of similar products, it also factors in, marketing campaigns and various other factors.

PRIMING The term Priming is defined as getting something ready for operation and can be used in a variety of situations.

PRIMING THE PUMP This term originally referred to old water pumps, where a suction valve had to be primed with water for the pump to work properly. It has now been adopted to refer to most situations where some initial activity is required to create some traction. In economies, activities such as an initial government spending plan, are seen as priming the pump to stimulate the economy. In sales, a quantity of initial can help stimulate traction in sales (In effect, priming the sales pump).

PRODUCT LANDING PAGE The Product Landing Page is primarily an online page that is designed to convert you to buy that product. There is usually an online Ad or email campaign to hook in prospective buyers and sending them to a webpage (The page they Land on) is a recognized sales strategy. Amazons Product pages are actually landing pages and provide some of the best sales conversion rates in the world.

PROFIT MARGIN   The difference between the purchase price (including any additional intermediary costs) and the profit left over after all sales costs are deducted.

R

RANKING   Traditionally a ranking is a relationship between two or more items (think of your top ten favourite songs of all time). In this book, ranking refers to the ranking of a product on amazon.com in relation to other products listed on Amazon.

RETURN ON INVESTMENT (R.O.I.)   A ratio calculating how much money was made on an investment as a percentage of the purchase price.

REVIEWS   In modern society it has become a recognized norm that we are expected to provide ratings for any business services that we receive. Whether we are rating our experience with Uber drivers or writing accommodation reviews (on the likes of TripAdvisor), we are becoming conditioned to do this. When we refer to reviews with regards to writing we are predominantly focused on the book reviews and ratings that are placed on book sites (such as Goodreads or Amazon.com). If we are looking for a coach to help us market books, we may want guidance on receiving reviews. These reviews can make a big difference between the quantities of our book sales.

REVIEWS (ALSO SHORT FOR CUSTOMER REVIEWS)
     Written feedback placed against your Amazon book listing (either positive or negative) that contributes to the ranking of your books' product listing.

S

SALES CONVERSION RATES   Marketing is a numbers game and not everyone who is exposed to marketing activities will proceed to make a purchase of that product. The term sales conversion rate relates to the number of people who are exposed to advertising or other marketing strategies and convert to actual buyers.

SCRIVENER   A commercially available word processing program (designed for authors) that allows you to organize documents, notes, and metadata while writing your book.

SIX DEGREES OF SEPARATION   This is a theory that any one person on the planet can be connected to another person on the planet via a chain of connections or acquaintances. The theory is that those acquaintances will total no more than five intermediaries and hence six degrees of separation.

T

TABLE OF CONTENTS   The table at the front of a book or publication that provides you with the location of chapter headings or major parts of the publication. In digital documents such as eBooks, this is usually full of hyperlinks to those locations.

TERMS OF SERVICE   In relation to Amazon the Terms of service are the rules and regulations that you must adhere to in order to buy or sell through the Amazon website. Individuals who have fallen foul of these rules when selling on Amazon have also had their ability to purchase other items from Amazon revoked.

THINKING OUTSIDE THE BOX This metaphor means to think differently or unconventionally. Although it can also be referred to as "Thinking out of the box", "Thinking outside of the square" or similar terms, the main premise of this term is novel or creative thinking.

TIME POOR A term that means what it says, you do not have enough time available to meet your requirements.

TRANSCRIPTION Transcription essentially means a written or printed version of something. For writers, it tends to mean the act of turning audio notes into written text. This conversion can be done by humans actually typing the audio recordings manually or software (such as Dragon professional) converting it automatically.

TWITTER (twitter.com) An online social networking service that enables users to send and receive messages no longer than 280 characters long.

U

UNIFORM RESOURCE LOCATOR *(URL)* A direct link to an online address. Usually displayed in blue font and underlined, clicking on this link takes you to a specific place on the internet. A form of hyperlink.

UPSOLD After a customer has chosen to make a purchase, they may be persuaded to buy something additional or more expensive. Being upsold can happen in a brick and mortar shop or during an online transaction.

UPWORK (Upwork.com) An online platform where you can hire freelancers to carry out almost any activity that can be performed by a computer.

W

WEBINAR   Simplistically a Webinar is a seminar conducted over the internet (abridged from the words Seminar and Worldwide web.

Y

YOUTUBE (Youtube.com)   A video sharing platform where you can create a video or view a video others have created. This platform has videos of everything from kittens playing the piano to instructions for you to build a cabin out of logs.

Annex C   A Tribute to the reader

A Tribute to You the reader

I hope that you have enjoyed reading this book as much as I've enjoyed writing it.

I'm sure that if you have worked through the chapters and exercises that you are now well on your journey to successfully publishing your book.

When I write my annual goals each year I include "To help others succeed" as one of my top goals.

If you have enjoyed this book please feel free to provide feedback with a review on Amazon (by following this link) so that I can reach more people and help even more people succeed.

About the Author

Ged Cusack is a Yorkshireman (Originally from Bradford in England), currently living in New Zealand.

His has a varied background encompassing 22 years as a British military engineer, several years in post-earthquake project management, Business coaching and many more ventures.

Growing up as a bit of a Nerd (before Geeks where cool) he has always loved to read and feels fortunate to now be able to produce something for others to read.

He is passionate about helping others succeed and providing as many resources as possible to make that happen.

Other Titles by this Author

Financial Freedom Beginners Guide Series		
	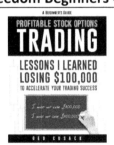	
FBA - Building an Amazon Business – The Beginner's Guide: Why and How to Build a Profitable Business on Amazon	**A Beginner's Guide Profitable Stock Options Trading**: Lessons I learned losing $100,000 to accelerate your trading success	**How to Choose a Writing Coach – A Beginner's Guide**: Ensuring your best chance for publishing success

The Inspiration Series	

Gratitude for Happiness: How to exercise your gratitude muscles	**527 Quotes for Entrepreneurs**: Providing Inspiration, Motivation, and Reflection

Annex D   Consolidated Exercises

Exercise One   Financial Spending

In this exercise I want you to determine how much discretionary spending that you have available, to commit to the publishing process.

As most of us now make our payments digitally, it can be relatively easy to review our bank and credit card statements to track our spending.

Here you are going to make a list of where you have previously allocated your income.

Apply the four categories below to each of the items in your list of expenditures:

A. Household Expenses
- Apply this to all of your monthly expenses (utilities, fuel etc.).
- Include your groceries here. If you regularly indulge in luxury items of food or drink, list those items under discretionary spending.

B. Business Expenses
- This may be easy to calculate. If you don't currently run a business it should be zero.

C. Savings
- You may have automated savings coming out of your income.
- As compound interest works best when you start to save early, I am not recommending that you stop contributing to your savings.

D. Discretionary Spending
- This includes any social spending but also any expenses that can be reduced (If an item isn't in one of the other three categories it should be here).
- If you have a mobile phone plan or a cable TV package can you reduce these costs?
- If you have credit card payments can you negotiate reduced payments?

The key here is that the sum total of these four figures should equal the total of all of your income.

People can either underestimate or overestimate the funds that they have available. By actually reviewing our current situation, it allows us to make educated decisions.

Once you have completed this exercise, it is up to you to prioritize what you choose to continue to use your funds for.

Exercise Two   Time Monitoring

For this exercise divide the next seven days into 15-minute segments and log your activities during each of those time-frames.

You can choose to track this in a spreadsheet or in a notebook but I encourage you to update this log as often as possible. There are productivity apps (such as "Focus Keeper") that allow you to set a timer for a 15 minute period. Feel free to use one of these if it helps you.

If you choose to list your activities at the end of each day (rather than regularly updating your log during the day) you may find it hard to remember how much time you devoted to each activity.

Rather than classifying your time into lots of sub-categories I find using the following five categories works best:

1. Work: This relates to any income generating activity.

2. Travel: This relates to travel to and from work so if you work from home this category may be redundant for you.

3. Eating: Although eating food is essential to living a two-hour lunch break is not necessarily the same thing. Therefore, log the time you actually spend eating. For a two-hour lunch, it may be 15 minutes of eating and the rest would be allocated under "other."

4. Sleep: We don't always understand how long we actually sleep so log your hours in bed resting (a midday snooze can also be logged here).

5. Other: I am not suggesting that the first four categories are the only important activities you undertake but sticking with just five categories will make it easier to update your log regularly. For anything in this category just write a one or two-word answer (such as Facebook, Netflix or date night).

At some time or another, you have probably heard the saying "there are never enough hours in a day." We all have the same 24 hours each day and by working through this exercise, you now have some idea where you allocate yours.

Exercise Three   Commitment
Now that you have determined where you spend your time and money, I want you to make a commitment to yourself.

Over the next twelve months, you need to determine how much you are prepared to commit to the publishing success of your book.

I have chosen twelve months as a benchmark as lots of people set annual goals (so find it easiest to plan for a year). If you have chosen to publish your book in less or more than a twelve month period then adjust your timescale.

As we all have different priorities you need to consider your personal circumstances and what will work for you before making a commitment.

- Financially - look at your discretionary spending budget and decide on a realistic amount to commit. You do not need to create a detailed financial business plan here. Just pick an amount and write it in a statement.
  e.g. "I am making a financial commitment to allocate $25 a week to the budget of my publishing success. "

- Time - look at the "Other" category of your available time and decide on a realistic amount to commit. Just pick an amount and write it in a statement.
  e.g. "I am making a commitment to allocate one hour every weekday (for the next six months) to the budget of my publishing success".

As I mentioned in the opportunity cost section, you need to balance your time and money expenditure. Once you've made these commitments they aren't set in stone. You can choose to monitor and adjust them as you proceed through the publishing process.

Exercise Four   Identifying Your Category

This exercise is geared at a manual strategy but if you choose to use a data analysis tool such as KDP Rocket, use that technique to choose your category faster.

- Search Amazon for the ten books that are closest to your book.
- Write down the categories and sub-categories of these books.
- Choose the two most common category strings.
- Note these categories for your future listing.

Remember that you may add further category strings after your book is live so take a note of the other category strings of the ten books.

If you can't find two common category strings from the first ten books you choose, keep searching similar books until you find them.

Exercise Five   Identifying the Top Books in Your Category

As you are starting on this writing journey you want to get the feel for the other books in the categories that you are writing.

Typing in a term such as "top 100 romance Novels" in Amazon's bookstore may give you varied results.

The Amazon Algorithm works on real-time data so the top 100 today may not be the top 100 tomorrow (if a new book suddenly has lots of sales).

For accurate data, I highly recommend purchasing or subscribing to analytical software but initially I just want you to get a feel for your competition.

In the Amazon Search box, choose kindle store from the drop-down menu and type in the box:

- Top 100 (insert your genre) books. If your book doesn't fall under an obvious genre (such as "Western Books" or "Romance") you may have to try a few different search terms.

You are going to look at the covers, titles and book descriptions in order to get a feel for those books before you proceed through this book.

As your search attempts can give you a variety of results I want you to use the following criteria to classify the books as your top five:

- The books with the highest number of reviews.
- The books with the lowest BSR (Best Seller Ranking).
- The books with the highest star rating for their reviews.
- The books that have a publication date within the last six months.

Although this criteria isn't all-encompassing it will give you an idea of what books are succeeding. Just pick the top two or three books and see if they are books that you would like to buy.

Exercise Six   Layout a Basic Launch Schedule
Plan out a basic Launch schedule for your first book. Use the table in Appendix C as your starting point or lay the schedule out using whatever format you are comfortable with. Remember to set your launch date and work backward.

Ensure that you include all of the elements of your book launch such as:

- The publication schedule
- Book editing
- The launch team
- Book cover
- etc etc.

Exercise Seven   Start to Build Your Email List Today
Start to build your email list (Ideally aim to have several hundred people on your list before you launch your book).

1. Choose an autoresponder provider such as:
- "Convertkit"
- "Mailerlite"
- "Mailchimp"

2. Choose a course or resource to guide you through the process of building your email list.

Some examples are:

- Pat Flynn
      https://www.smartpassiveincome.com/email-list-strategies/
- Ryan Levesque   https://www.askmethod.com/
- Nathalie Lussier   https://nathalielussier.com/

If you aren't comfortable with any of the resources listed above, just type "How to build an email list" in a google search and you will find a multitude of options.

Don't delay, pick a resource that you feel comfortable with and begin to build your list

There is no shortage of opportunities to help you build your list and if the voice in your head is telling you, "it's too soon to build a list", it's a liar!

Exercise Eight   Determine the Format for Writing Your Book
You can choose Scrivener MS Word, Google docs etc. but I suggest that you decide from the offset which you will use.

221

Although we are in the early stages of your book, for efficiency it is best to start with the end in mind. You may change certain things as you work through the process but the exercises below are designed to help provide you an overview and starting point.

Rather than just decide how you will write your book, you need to take some action.

Some options for those actions are:

- Open a folder on your computer and start to populate it with MS Word docs & a tracking spreadsheet.
- Create a Google account and Open a google doc & a Google sheet in your Google drive.
- Purchase Scrivener & Open a new project in Scrivener for your book.

Whichever format you decide to use, don't make a decision without taking some action. Before you leave this exercise, carry out at least two tasks (relating to this format) to move your book forward.

Exercise Nine   Determine your Research Process
Whether you are writing Fiction or Non-Fiction you will need to have some methods for research.

Although your budget may be a big determining factor in which method you use, here are some Suggestions:

- Research all of your content through online searches.
- Research all of your content through books.
- Research all of your content by traveling and interacting with people.
- Research your content using a hybrid of all of the options above (If you are choosing this option, determine what percentage of each of the methods you will use to produce your content).

Whichever research process you decide to use, don't make a decision without taking some action. You will need to track your research so set up a tracking system for this research, before leaving this exercise.

Exercise Ten   Determine your Editing Process

You need to decide if you need all four types of editor for your book and consider where you will source any relevant editors.

Points to consider:

- What is your Editing budget?
- Who do you know that may edit at a discount?
- Do you have anyone who would provide a final proofread for you?
- How much notice will your editors /proof-readers require before your publishing deadline?

Before you leave this exercise, write down which of the four types of editing that you are going to employ. For each of the types of editing that you decide to use, write down two sources or options that you will use to achieve this edit.

Exercise Eleven   Writing a Brief for an Existing Book Cover

Search on Amazon in your current book genre and choose a specific book cover from those listed.

Using the template and sample briefs in Appendix E, complete a brief for the designer of this book cover.

As you already have the completed book cover as a reference this should be easier than designing your own cover from your own imagination.

- Identify where the title ends and the sub-title starts.
- Take a screenshot of similar book covers in this genre and look for commonalities.
- For any colours search the web for a colour chart and pick the closest code to that colour (quoting the code and screenshotting the chart).

Exercise Twelve   Writing a Brief for Your Book Cover
Now that you are more experienced with the process of cover design, you can start to work on your own book cover.

Using the template and sample briefs in Appendix E, complete a brief for the designer for your own book cover.

- If you have already completed your initial design for your book cover you may want to work through this exercise to see if you have missed anything.
- Ensure your book cover is relevant to your genre.

NB. *Don't let your search for the perfect cover stop you publishing your book.*

Exercise Thirteen   Choosing a Working Title
Choose a working title for your book. Although you probably have some vague title when you refer to your work, just calling it "The Book" is not very productive.

Choosing something a little closer to the subject matter of the book can help keep you on track with the premise of the book (subject matter). Calling your book "How to make $30,000 from property flipping" or "The tale of the dragon who became a princess" will keep the main subject of the book, front of mind.

Exercise Fourteen   Beta Testing Your Book Titles

Narrow your book title down to three options and then ask for feedback on which title is more likely to pique reader's interest.

- You can test the titles by asking for feedback or setting up a survey on Twitter, Facebook or some other social media platform.
- Ensure that you write the titles in the same font type and size, to avoid variations unduly influencing respondents.
- Try to test your titles in audiences that may read this genre of book.
- Choose the title with the highest feedback. If the top two are close then carry out another test with just those top two titles.

Exercise Fifteen   Practicing With HTML

Choose six books in your genre, ideally, three written by well-known authors and three by not so famous authors.

I am assuming that if you are writing in a genre it is one that you traditionally read so you will know the big name authors in your genre. If not pick the top six books based on the number of reviews that they have.

- Pick at least one of these listings that hasn't been formatted with bold headings, bullet points, etc. and copy and paste the text into an HTML generator.
- Format the text a few times and copy and paste the code that the generator provides into a separate document.

This practice will make you comfortable using the tool and make it less daunting when you come to format your own text.

Exercise Sixteen   Confirming Your Keywords

It is important to remember that you are looking for additional keywords to those in your book title.

Although you are only provided seven keyword spaces in your Amazon listing, that does not mean that you are limited to only seven words. You can add short Search terms up to 60 characters in each box.

- Consider sentences and phrases that describe or portray the content of your book.
- In the Amazon search bar type in the first word of those sentences and observe the options that the autofill function provides.
- Make a list of these phrases and choose seven for your listing.

Keep the list of the phrases that you don't use for future testing and Amazon Ads.

Exercise Seventeen   The Twenty Hooks List

Write twenty separate hooks for your book description.

Remember that your hook is the first words they will see in your book description so craft it well.

Here's a refresher of some of my previous tips when writing your hook:

- Try to complete your hook in around twenty words.
- Don't exceed thirty words.
- For Non-Fiction
  - Start the hook off with a question (address the reader's pain point), why are they looking for your book.
  - Ensure you include a solution to their pain point in the hook. How will your book solve their problem?

- For Fiction paint a picture that will entice the reader into your world. Confirm that your book is taking them where the book cover and title promised.
- Check out your competitor's listings (the top books in your niche or genre).
- Once you have twenty versions of your hook, survey the top three to see which is more appealing to readers. Ask "which description is more likely to get people to buy the book" rather than "which do you like best".

One last point here, you may see that some of the top traditionally published authors don't have well laid out and appealing book descriptions. Their publishers have probably spent a lot of money on marketing and don't feel it's necessary. This is where you have an advantage over them.

Exercise Eighteen   Pick a Comparative Listing Price
Choose 6 similar books to your books, length, and subject matter notoriety (don't choose a best seller in your niche/genre).

Aim for books with a BSR from 30,000 to 50,000.

To ensure that you are comparing books at a similar level ensure that they are similar in the following aspects:

- The number of pages.
- The number of reviews.
- How long the book has been published.
- How many formats the book is available in.

Choose a comparative price for your books list price.

Exercise Nineteen   Determine the Price Stages of Your Book
You can change your list prices at any time but here are a few suggestions for some of your price points:

- The Pre-order price — if you intend to use this KDP function, you may choose to make the price difference between this and the initial list price attractive.
- Your initial list— if you aren't using Pre-orders remember that this may be quite low (to get some early reviews).
- The Post promotion price — prior to the Countdown Deals you are not allowed to have a lower price for the previous thirty days. For an initial launch countdown deal, you may have started your listing at a higher price point. For subsequent countdown deals in the future, you may decide to increase your price to $3.99 or $4.99.
- The Appealing Kindle Unlimited (KU) price — remember that you want to optimize your book value to KU readers. If you decide to subscribe to KDPS at a later date you may want to revise your list price first.

Exercise Twenty   Install Book Report
Once your book has gone live on KDP, login to https://www.getbookreport.com and install the Book Report tool to your Bookmarks Bar

I have no affiliation with this site and this exercise is just a suggestion to help you understand the reports on your KDP account.

Exercise Twenty One   Setup your Amazon Associate Account
If you haven't set up your website yet, then come back to this later but:
- Ensure that you have affiliate links to your books on your website.

- Ensure that you put affiliate links to your other books in your published books.

If you don't have a website you can't currently join this program but as an author aiming to maximize income, I suggest you may want to do this.

Exercise Twenty Two   Have a Good Quality Picture Taken of Yourself

Ideally, you want to provide continuity so you will likely be using the same image of yourself in various places.

Points to bear in mind:

- With the availability and quality of cameras on our smartphones, we should all be able to get great pictures but ensure that they are of a good quality.
- It's surprising how inexpensive it can be for a couple of pictures but if Cashflow is an issue there are less expensive ways to get quality pictures.

Contact tutors at your local college or high school, their students may be glad of the experience (and should have access to modern equipment).

Exercise Twenty Three   Write Two Versions of Your Bio

Have a couple of versions of your bio available. For most marketing or promotional sites, they will want information about you. As they may have limited space for your information, you may need to abridge your initial bio.

Don't change the information that your bio contains, as you are still targeting the same market.

For this exercise just produce a long and short version of your bio.

- Create one Bio 400 words long.
- Create one Bio 800 words long.

By having two different lengths of your bio readily available, you can quickly adapt them to meet future requirements.

Exercise Twenty Four   Write a Book synopsis

Having a synopsis for your book available in various lengths will save you time later. As with your bio, marketing activities may provide limited space for your book synopsis.

For this exercise produce three versions of the synopsis for the same book.

- Create one synopsis 100 words long.
- Create one synopsis 200 words long.
- Create one synopsis 300 words long.

This exercise provides you with three versions of your synopsis but can also help with the formulation of the description for your book listing.

Exercise Twenty Five   Choose Ten Free Sites to Contact for Your Book Launch

Determine what you will need to supply them prior to your promotion (and have it ready):

- Do they just need your promo dates?
- Do they need a book synopsis (100,200 or 300 words)?
- Do they need a short author bio?
- Do they need a jpeg of the book cover (or will they get the info from your Amazon ASIN)?

- Do they need a specific number of days' notice to list your book promotion?

Doing this preparation now will help you immensely when your book is finally ready to launch.

Exercise Twenty Six   Choose Ten Paid Sites That You Will Contact for Your Book Launch

Bookbub.com and the likes may be above your budget but even some of the free sites have a paid option.

The paid option guarantees that they will list your promotion and can be relatively cheap.

- Look at the requirements that you prepared for the free promotions.
- Determine if you need to supply any extra information for a paid promotion.
- Ensure you have met all of their requirements.

Doing this preparation now will help you immensely when your book is finally ready to launch.

Exercise Twenty Seven   Choose a Giveaway or Countdown Deal

Although you may be some distance from your book launch, this simple exercise will make you review the information on the two options and save you time come launch time.

You can always change your mind later but at least you'll have more insight into these two options at that time. If you are close to launch then you can actually schedule your Promotion now.

Choose your preference:

- The Countdown deal.
- The Giveaway promotion $0.99.

The KDP site provides plenty of advice and instructions to carry out one of these promotions. Just pick which one you are going to do.

Exercise Twenty Eight   Compile a Keyword List for Your Sponsored Ad
For your first sponsored Ad you should start with 100-300 Keywords,

The easiest way to compile your list is to use software such as KDP Rocket but if you are on a limited budget you might want to use the manual option.

Unlike the seven keywords in your book listing, you can use other author's names in your Ad keywords.

Some keyword suggestions:

- The names of authors with similar books.
- The names of books in the same genres.
- The types of sentences people would type in when looking for books in your genre.

Ensure that you choose close matches as if your keywords are aimed at the wrong readers it can disappoint and annoy them.

Exercise Twenty Nine   Set Your Advertising Budget
From the chapter on commitment you will be aware of your available capital.

From the money that you have available, determine how much you will commit to your marketing budget.

- This doesn't have to be a huge amount but you have to start somewhere.
- Ideally budget for an ongoing monthly amount.
- Commit to an initial minimum amount and ensure that you keep to it.

As you work through a campaign your budget may change but this exercise will give you a starting point.

Exercise Thirty   Calculate the Royalties for Your Book
From the pricing chapter, you should now have determined the initial price for your book.

I realize that you may have to deduct taxes and other considerations from your royalties but I just want you to set a baseline here.

Sometimes authors are surprised at the small amount of royalties that they receive for their book. For the purpose of this exercise, you are going to calculate the amount of hard cash you will get for the sale of your book.

A. Assume that you are receiving 70% Royalties.
- Multiply the price of your book by 70 and divide it by 100 to get your 70% royalties.
B. Assume that you are receiving 30% Royalties.
- Multiply the price of your book by 30 and divide it by 100 to get your 70% royalties.

I know that this is a simple exercise but lots of authors focus on the writing and sometimes forget about the money.

It can be quite sobering when you look at these numbers.

Exercise Thirty One   Schedule the Production of Your Print Book

Don't let the fact that your print book isn't ready stop you launching your first kindle book.

Ensure that you have a timetable and take into account:

- The extra time, cost and skill for editing.
- The need for a full book cover (not just a jpeg for your eBook front).
- The text for the back of your book (this is another chance to market your book).

Even if you are only planning to launch your print book a few weeks after your digital book, remain flexible.

Annex E   Book Launch Checklist

To get the most benefits from this Checklist, you should view the successful publication of your book as a project.

Depending on your current skillsets (and to some extent how much of a perfectionist that you are), some of the activities below may need more or less time.

This checklist is designed to provide a comprehensive overview of the activities required for a successful book launch. Start with the end in mind, before you even write a word of your book.

The steps are laid out in a logical order for the publishing process but it is suggested that you read the whole list before you start to plan out your launch.

If you complete some tasks out of order, it's not an issue. Be happy that you have completed any task.

It might seem a bit daunting when you look at all of the activities here, but that is why you have the checklist. If you find it easier to schedule with a spreadsheet or other software, feel free to copy and paste the contents of these tables.

Step	Element	Activities	Est Comp Date	Comp Date
1	Budget	Confirmed time available for this publishing project.		
		Confirmed time allocated for this publishing project.		
		Confirmed finances available for this publishing project.		
		Confirmed finances allocated for this publishing project.		
		Reviewed the opportunity costs of this project (Balancing time & financial budgets).		

Step	Element	Activities	Est Comp Date	Comp Date
2	Niche / Genre	Confirmed the subject of book (fiction / non-fiction). Are you solving a problem (if non-fiction)?		
		Confirmed niche or genre (using google searches).		
		Confirmed Amazon categories.		
		Confirmed working title for the book.		

Step	Element	Activities	Est Comp Date	Comp Date
3	Email Lists	Confirmed (and created) content for opt-ins.		
		Subscribed to an email marketing platform.		
		Setup Landing Page.		

Step	Element	Activities	Est Comp Date	Comp Date
4	Social Media	Chosen three social media platforms to focus on.		
		Setup three social media profiles.		
		Scheduled a social media content posting schedule.		
		Built some social currency.		
		Scheduled the build of an Author website.		

Step	Element	Activities	Est Comp Date	Comp Date
5	Book Content	Confirmed current subject knowledge.		
		Confirmed info required.		
		Scheduled research.		
		Scheduled content production.		

Step	Element	Activities	Est Comp Date	Comp Date
6	Publication Schedule	Launch date chosen.		
		Publication date chosen.		
		Manuscript upload date chosen.		
		Pre-order start date chosen.		
		Launch, the point of no return date chosen (can be between the publication and the launch date).		
		Updated manuscript (with a link to its Amazon review page) uploaded.		
		KDP Giveaway or Countdown deal scheduled.		

Step	Element	Activities	Est Comp Date	Comp Date
7	Book Editing	Scheduled development edit.		
		Schedule substantive edit.		
		Schedule copy edit.		
		Schedule proofreading.		
		Schedule KDP upload.		
		Arc distribution dates chosen.		

Step	Element	Activities	Est Comp Date	Comp Date
8	Launch Team	Sourced launch team.		
		Built Facebook page for the book launch.		
		Scheduled contact frequency for launch team.		

Step	Element	Activities	Est Comp Date	Comp Date
9	Book Synopsis	Compiled twenty initial hooks for the book listing.		
		Chosen the hook for the book listing.		
		Compiled the rest of the book listing.		
		Sent synopsis to launch team.		
		Edited synopsis for 100, 200 & 300 word options.		

Step	Element	Activities	Est Comp Date	Comp Date
10	KDP Account	Set up KDP account (including tax interview).		

Step	Element	Activities	Est Comp Date	Comp Date
11	Book Title / Subtitle	Created three options for the book title (Using amazon keyword searches for subtitles).		
		Split-tested titles with launch team.		
		Final book title confirmed (ensuring the text is readable in thumbnail).		

Step	Element	Activities	Est Comp Date	Comp Date
12	Book Cover	Reviewed competitor's book covers (focus on design, font & colour).		
		Compiled draft brief for cover designer.		
		Tasked designer with three cover options.		
		Split-tested cover options with launch team.		
		Tasked designer with any modifications.		
		Book cover uploaded to KDP.		

Step	Element	Activities	Est Comp Date	Comp Date
13	Book Listing	Reviewed the book descriptions (on Amazon) of the top ten books in the same category.		
		Created a compelling book listing (using book synopsis & formatting with HTML).		
		Chosen the initial seven keywords for the book listing.		
		Confirmed 1st book category.		
		Confirmed 2nd book category.		
		Updated all info for book listing on KDP.		

Step	Element	Activities	Est Comp Date	Comp Date
14	Amazon Book Reviews	Scheduled pre-launch review activities (with launch team).		
		Scheduled post-launch review activities.		
		Universal book link created for book marketing.		
		Scheduled ongoing review activities.		
		Listed promotion details on book promotion sites.		

Step	Element	Activities	Est Comp Date	Comp Date
15	Book Pricing	Reviewed the price of competitor's books on Amazon.		
		Determined book pre-order price.		
		Determined book launch price.		
		Determined post-launch book price.		

Step	Element	Activities	Est Comp Date	Comp Date
16	Author Media Pack	Author website build complete.		
		Scheduled book video recording.		
		Recorded book promo video.		
		Uploaded video to social media profiles.		
		Uploaded video to Amazon author central page.		
		Author biography (Bio) completed and reviewed.		
		Uploaded author bio to your website & other social media accounts.		
		Uploaded bio to author central page.		

Step	Element	Activities	Est Comp Date	Comp Date
17	Amazon Display Ads	Determined ideal reader (using niche/genre choice).		
		Chosen text for Amazon Ad.		
		Scheduled Ad start & end dates (No Ads started until 15-20 reviews).		

Step	Element	Activities	Est Comp Date	Comp Date
18	Amazon Sponsored Ads	Compiled a list of 100-300 keywords (including other authors and book titles).		
		Chosen text for Ad.		
		Scheduled Ad start & end dates (No Ads started until 15-20 reviews).		

Annex F   Book Review Activities Checklist

The search for Amazon Book Reviews can sometimes feel like Indiana Jones's quest for the Holy Grail.

Although there are no magic solutions to get every book (you publish) a bucket load of 5-star reviews, the activities listed below will improve your chances.

If you are a person who likes statistics, I'll warn you in advance that the chances of you getting a review from 100% of the people who purchase your book are close to 0%.

	Activities	Est Comp Date	Comp Date
1	Set up email list opt-ins.		

An email list is invaluable for all business owners, especially Indie authors. If you haven't started your email list yet, it is never too early. Plant the seeds for the relationship with your subscribers and they are more likely to review your books.

I know that most authors are paranoid that if they have any connection with another person on the planet Amazon will not allow them to review their book. With globalization, it is hard to find someone that you do not have some digital connection.

You can't have anyone in your immediate family, leave a review but you need some initial reviews so your email list is a goldmine.

Activities		Est Comp Date	Comp Date
2	Build a book launch team.		

Humans instinctively don't like to be the first to do something and this Catch 22 means that you need some initial reviews in order to get reviews.

If you have already built a launch team for Beta reading, then utilize them for some initial reviews. If you haven't built a launch team yet, start building a team as soon as possible, in preparation for your book launch.

This team should be prepared to place the first reviews of your book.

Activities		Est Comp Date	Comp Date
3	Distribute book Advanced Review Copies (ARCs).		

Traditionally publishers used to send out advance print copies of a book to selective readers in advance of the book launch (to get early reviews in newspapers etc.).

These pre-launch copies became known as Advanced Review Copies (ARCs) and the name has remained through to the digital age. With digital Book formats such as Pdfs, Mobi, and Epub etc., the distribution costs are minimal so you can send out a lot more copies.

ARCs do not have to be limited to pre-launch activities. You can continue to use them after the launch.

Include the distribution of ARCs of your book as part of your ongoing marketing plan (in order to promote book reviews).

Activities		Est Comp Date	Comp Date
4	Add universal links to your manuscript for your book's amazon review page.		

With our ever-diminishing attention span, statistics show that when someone has to click twice to make a purchase (that second click is enough that), they are more likely to abandon the purchase.

Basically, humans are getting lazier!

One of the benefits that a Kindle book has over a physical product, is that you can actually ask nicely for a review within the book (product) and create a link directly to your book's review page.

Remember that the purpose of this link is to make it easier for readers to leave a review. Getting readers to log in to Amazon and find their order and then place a review can seem like too much trouble, for even the most ardent fan.

Having a link that they can click on, while they're reading your book (that takes them straight to that books review page) is a lot more convenient.

	Activities	Est Comp Date	Comp Date
5	List your books on your author website.		

By listing your books on your own author website and driving traffic there, you are helping to build more of a relationship with your readers. As people visit your website they can see that you are more than just one book.

As only a small number of readers will review your book, they are more likely to leave a review for someone that they feel invested in, rather than some random author whose book they have read.

	Activities	Est Comp Date	Comp Date
6	Subscribe to review groups.		

There are some very supportive groups online for authors but a lot of these groups stipulate that they do not allow self-promotion. If your focus is to get book reviews it makes sense to join specific groups, that allow or actively display promoting your book for reviews.

These groups exist on Facebook, Promotion websites etc. and as they include words like "Kindle Reviews" or "Book Reviews) in the group titles, it is pretty easy to determine which groups to join.

	Activities	Est Comp Date	Comp Date
7	Create contests and send them to your email list.		

There are various ways to provide copies of your book for reviews but creating contests can help keep engagement with your email list. A physical copy as a prize, can sometimes provide a greater chance of reviews.

You can also create contests on Facebook and other social media platforms as a way of promoting your books.

Although there is no definite expectation that winners of your book will provide a review, the fact that they received a gift tends to increase your chances that they will leave a review.

	Activities	Est Comp Date	Comp Date
8	Promote your book while networking (always ask for reviews).		

You may be surprised by the number of authors who meet readers of their book while they are networking. You'll probably be more surprised by the number of authors who forget to ask the reader to leave a review on Amazon.

One thing to note is that not everyone knows how to leave a book review.

Have you have ever left a networking event with a business card and later realized that you couldn't remember much about the person on the card? Rather than expecting a reader to remember to leave a review, follow up with that reader later with instructions (and a link to your books review page), telling them how to leave a review for your book on Amazon.

Always remember to ask a reader for a review of your book.

	Activities	Est Comp Date	Comp Date
9	Schedule an amazon five day giveaway.		

I know that it can feel odd, giving away an unlimited number of digital copies of your work for free. Yes, you have worked hard to produce this book but you are not giving it away indefinitely.

Think how many large retailers have deals like Buy One Get One Free? They wouldn't be doing this if it wasn't a successful marketing tool.

Activities		Est Comp Date	Comp Date
10	Schedule Amazon countdown deals.		

Initially, the Amazon Free giveaways were a novelty and converted to more book reviews. It's worth noting that even though the books are free, the reviews that they produce are classed as verified reviews.

Because free stuff doesn't have as much perceived value (lots of readers download free kindle books and don't even open them), $0.99 may be now classed as the new "FREE".

Although Amazon Giveaways may receive more downloads than Amazon Countdown deals, the conversion rate for Countdown deals (from download to review) can be higher.

Rather than trying to determine which is the best option, alternate between the two.

Activities		Est Comp Date	Comp Date
11	List your book promotions on promotion sites.		

Whether you are using an Amazon giveaway or a Countdown deal, ensure that you list your promotion on as many promotion sites as possible.

The wider you share your promotion the greater the potential for downloads and the more chance of reviews.

Some of these sites need ten days' notice to list your promotion, so ensure that you allow yourself plenty of planning time before your promotion.

	Activities	Est Comp Date	Comp Date
12	Launch a Goodreads giveaway.		

Since Goodreads started charging for their giveaways, they have included extras for authors (such as a reminder for readers to review your book.

Based on my own experiences (and that of other authors), the results here can be varied.

Although you can't guarantee a five-star rating or that a reader will even review a book from a Goodreads giveaway, this is an opportunity to get your book in front of readers on a site that is full of readers.

The more readers, the better chance you have of getting reviews.

	Activities	Est Comp Date	Comp Date
13	Update content for new editions.		

When you update more than 10% of the content of your book on Amazon you can list it as a new edition.

Anyone who has previously downloaded a kindle version of your book is now contacted by Amazon and offered the new edition for FREE. You have suddenly put yourself back in the front of the minds of your readers and increase your chance of getting more reviews.

	Activities	Est Comp Date	Comp Date
14	Post weekly social media review requests.		

You can schedule these requests in advance. Just asking regularly "if anyone has read my book, would you please leave a review", is a simple option to jog reader's memory.

If you have more than one book, send a separate message (tweet etc.) for each book. Ensure that you include a link to the books Amazon review page in that message.

Remember that you should try to make it as easy as possible for readers to leave a review.

	Activities	Est Comp Date	Comp Date
15	Contact book bloggers with review requests.		

There are lots of book bloggers out there and they receive lots of requests to review books.

To have the best chance of getting your book reviewed here are a few tips:

- Build up a relationship with bloggers before asking for a review. Comment on some of their posts, follow them on other social media platforms etc.
- Specifically approach bloggers who review books in your genre.
- Tailor your approach (familiarize yourself with some of their other reviews), mention things you liked about their other reviews.
- If they reply that they are currently not accepting books, ask permission to contact them again and ask when would be a good time to contact them. Leave the door open and get a specific date for your next contact.
- Contact multiple bloggers to increase your odds of one accepting you.
- Log all contacts and schedule the next contact to ensure that you use your time efficiently.
- If a blogger has reviewed one of your books, remember to approach them, prior to your next book launch.

If you are fortunate to get a book reviewed remember to thank the blogger.

Activities		Est Comp Date	Comp Date
16	Ask for reviews in any Ads or blog posts on your website.		

Whether you are boosting a Facebook post or receiving comments on a blog, treat it as networking and remember to ask for a review.

Ensure that your review request is relevant (e.g. if you publish in Sci-Fi Fantasy and Non-Fiction Biographies, don't paste a review request for one on a post for the other).

NB.   Remember that if you do not ask for a review, your odds of getting a review are decreased.

Annex G   Book Cover Designer Briefs

In this Annex, I am going to supply you a couple of examples of the kind of briefs that I prepare before I contact a designer.

Although some designers can accept your (pre-prepared) brief in its current format, a lot of the larger designers have their own template layout for speed and efficiency. You can cut and paste a lot of the information from your brief into the designer's template.

Designer Templates

Different designers tend to ask for similar information but have their templates laid out in a different order.

As you don't normally get to see the templates before you have paid your $10 I have provided a couple of examples of the layouts of templates I have been provided in the past.

With each of the templates, I have also provided a Sample brief (completed template) to help you to prepare your own brief in advance:

Template 1
1. What industry does this order relate to? (Optional).
2. When I submit an order back to you, you must click "Request Revision" so the order goes into my queue for edits, not clicking this your order will autocomplete.
3. Book Title and Sub-title.
4. Author Name.
5. Design preferences:

- Do you have any color preferences?
- Do you have any covers that you like the style of (provide links here)?
6. Do you have any customer artwork:
- Provide author photos (optional).
- Provide sample artwork or book covers to mimic.
7. Do you have any stock photographs:
- If you haven't uploaded a photo but have seen a stock photo that you would like us to use, please provide the 8-9 digit number.
- You may decide to let us choose a stock photo but most authors have an image already in mind.

8 Required for print covers (Createspace etc.):
- Book size.
- Final Page Count.
- Back cover Text.
- ISBN number if you have it.

Template 2
1. What industry does this order relate to? (Optional).
2. Color preferences (if any).
3. Dimensions of the cover (if not Amazon standard e-book size, be specific about the size in inches or pixels).
4. Images for the cover:
- Please pick a photo/graphic from 888888.com (send us the link or ID number and we'll purchase it).
- We will not choose a picture for you, because of the way that we work.
5. Text on the cover (title, author, subtitle).
6. Send links, attachments or names of a few books that you like the design of.

Designer Sample Briefs

Book Cover Brief 1
Hi***

1. I would like you to provide a book cover design for my new book (insert book title & sub-title):
- The book genre is *******
- I have included an image of ******* that I would like to include on the cover.
- The rough design provided is only an example and I encourage you to provide some creative input.
2. Please find attached examples of some of the book covers for the (bestselling books) in this genre.

Aspects of these covers that I like are:
- The Clean font of the book title, that makes it easy to read.
3. I have also attached a copy of a couple of my other book covers so that you can see the kind of brand that I am trying to promote. Some of the criteria in my current covers:
- The use of a lot of white space.
- The layout of the title at the top, a small image and the sub-title underneath.
- The presence of the color [insert your color] as the main color.
4. Greyscale

A high percentage of Kindle readers' purchase on their Kindle (from a black and white thumbnail image):
- It is therefore important that there is enough dark/light color contrast.
- The text and the images on the cover must be legible in black and white.
5. The specifications for the finished cover (as per KDP requirements) are:
- To be in jpeg format.
- The Ratio of the width to height of the image is to be 1:6.
- Minimum size is 2813 x 4500 pixels.

NB.   When you are publishing your first book you may not have a full idea of the kind of book cover or brand that you are trying to produce so I have provided an example of a shorter brief here.

Book Cover Brief 2

Hi [insert name of Designer]

1. I would like you to provide a book cover design for my new book (insert book title & sub-title):
- The book genre is [insert genre].
2. Please find attached examples of some of the book covers for (the bestselling) books in this genre.
3. I invite you to be creative and provide a cover in a similar vein.
4. Colors Greyscale.

A high percentage of Kindle readers' purchase on their Kindle (from a black and white thumbnail image):
- Please use similar colors to the samples provided, but only a maximum of two colors in total (not including black and white.
- It is very important that there is enough dark/light color contrast.
- The text and the images on the cover must be legible in black and white.
5. The specifications for the finished cover (as per KDP requirements) are:
- To be in jpeg format.
- The Ratio of the width to height of the image is to be 1:6.
- Minimum size is 2813 x 4500 pixels.

N.B.   Be aware that some of the bigger design companies on Fiverr will have different variations of this layout for you to complete. Although you will have to enter your information in a different order than the way it is laid out above, you will save a lot of time by already having the information prepared in advance.

Lightning Source UK Ltd.
Milton Keynes UK
UKHW020626191022
410722UK00008B/223